A Deeper Love

ELIZABETH SMITH retired from teaching in 1988 and founded Contemplative Outreach UK the following year. She has given retreats and workshops all over England, Scotland, and Wales on Centering Prayer and the Christian contemplative tradition. She is married with two adult children and lives in Preston, Lancashire.

FR JOSEPH CHALMERS, O.CARM., comes from Glasgow and is Prior General of the Carmelite Order. He has extensive experience in giving retreats and served as Prior of Aylesford and Provincial of the Carmelites in Britain before his election to his present position in September 1995, which requires him to live in Rome. He worked with Mrs Smith on Centering Prayer retreats and workshops from 1990.

Both authors are members of the International Faculty of Contemplative Outreach, which is the group responsible for maintaining the integrity of the message of Centering Prayer and for overseeing the development of retreats and workshops.

A DEEPER LOVE

An Introduction to Centering Prayer

ELIZABETH SMITH
JOSEPH CHALMERS

CONTINUUM • NEW YORK

First published in Great Britain in 1999 by
BURNS & OATES,
Wellwood, North Farm Road,
Tunbridge Wells, Kent TN2 3DR

First published in the United States of America in 1999 by
The Continuum Publishing Company
370 Lexington Avenue, New York, NY 10017

Library of Congress Cataloging in Publication Data

Smith, Elizabeth.
    A deeper love : an introduction to centering prayer / Elizabeth
Smith, Joseph Chalmers.
      p.   cm.
    ISBN 0-8264-1210-6 (pbk.)
    1.   Contemplation.   I. Chalmers, Joseph.   II. Title.
BV5091.C7S58   1999
248.3—dc21   99-17592
                                                CIP

Typeset by Shelleys The Printers, Sherborne
Printed in Great Britain by
Biddles Limited, Guildford and King's Lynn

Contents

Foreword

Elizabeth Smith, Director of Contemplative Outreach U.K., and the Most Reverend Joseph Chalmers, O. Carm., Prior General of the Carmelite Order, have collaborated in providing an excellent summary of the conceptual background of Centering Prayer and the Christian contemplative journey as found in my three books: *Open Mind, Open Heart; The Mystery of Christ;* and *Invitation to Love.* The instruction and guidance contained in these pages are the necessary follow-up to the Introductory Workshop in Centering Prayer. Especially in areas where the above-mentioned trilogy is hard to obtain, readers can find here a synthesis that has been painstakingly and accurately crafted and which includes all the essential information in a single book. I am deeply grateful to the authors.

Thomas Keating, O.C.S.O.
Snowmass, Colorado, 11 June 1998

Authors' Preface

This book has come out of our experience of teaching, but above all practising, Centering Prayer over a number of years. Both of us have found it helpful in our own lives and we wish simply to share it with others. Much of what we have written is based on the insights of Fr Thomas Keating, an American Trappist monk, who founded Contemplative Outreach in the USA in order to teach Centering Prayer in the context of the Christian contemplative tradition and to support those who take up this way of prayer.

We wish to make the writings of Thomas Keating more widely known because we believe he has much to offer to those who desire to respond wholeheartedly to the invitation of Christ to enter into an intimate relationship with God. This simple introductory book, we believe, may be of help to those who are searching.

May all who read this book be inspired to continue to consent to the presence and action of God in their lives. Our prayer for you is that of St Paul:

> This then is what I pray kneeling before the Father from whom every family whether spiritual or natural takes its name, that out of his infinite glory you may be strengthened within through the working of the Spirit. May Christ live in your hearts through faith and may charity be the root and foundation of your life. In this way with all the saints you will grasp the breadth and the length, the height and the depth of the love of Christ which is beyond all knowledge until you are filled with the utter fullness of God.
>
> To the One whose power working in us can do infinitely more than we could ask for or even imagine, to God be glory in the church and in Christ Jesus for all generations world without end. Amen" (Eph. 3:14-21).

Chapter One

PRAYER AS RELATIONSHIP

There are many different ways of praying, and each way is valuable so long as it brings us into contact with God. What matters is that we actually pray, because it is through prayer that we relate to God. Each of us has been called and given the power to respond to the invitation to an intimate relationship with God. Jesus promised that in those who keep his word he and the Father would make their home (John 14:23). He does not want us to remain simply disciples but to become friends—"I do not call you servants any longer, because the servant does not know what the master is doing; but I have called you friends, because I have made known to you everything that I have heard from my Father" (John 15:15). We are called then into a relationship with Christ. The purpose of this relationship is that we go out and bear fruit, fruit that will last (John 15:16). The more we become like Christ, the more fruitful will our lives be.

If we are to grow in our relationship with Christ and indeed become his friends we need to learn as much as we can about how to relate. Jesus proclaimed that the second commandment, to love our neighbour, was like the first, to love God with our whole heart and soul (Matt. 22:38-9). The new commandment he left his disciples was that they love one another as he had loved them (John 13:34). We can learn much from our ordinary human relationships. We are changed by our relationships. In some sense we become like those we love, so as the Spirit draws us into a deeper relationship with Christ we become transformed and therefore more like him. There is of course an important difference between our

11

relationship with Christ and our human relationships, a difference that is central to an adequate understanding of Christian spirituality. In this relationship Christ is always the initiator. We can go to Christ because he has first called us and drawn us to himself. Any movement toward Christ, any movement toward good, occurs because of the presence and action of the Spirit. We can search for God only because we have been already found by God. Clearly we have a crucial role in the relationship because we are free to ignore the promptings of the Spirit and act contrary to them. No single model can completely define God's relationship with us but one way that may be helpful is to look at how we grow in ordinary human relationships and then apply that same process to our participation in the life of God.

As in any relationship there are various levels of intimacy, and we are free to choose and remain at whatever level with which we are comfortable. We all have the right to remain within our own boundaries. We have the right to say "thus far and no further!" and to choose to limit the self-revelation that a growing intimacy demands. In very broad terms we could say there are four levels of human relationship—acquaintanceship, friendliness, friendship, and intimacy. We shall look at each stage and see how a relationship normally develops, keeping in mind that our human relationships can be a mirror for our relationship with God.

1. Acquaintanceship

Imagine the situation where a handsome young man spies a beautiful young woman across a crowded room. He is attracted to her and begins to make his way toward her. She pretends not to notice his approach but she has already taken in his interest and indeed welcomes it. She would not mind at all getting to know him. When he arrives in front of the young woman, they begin an animated conversation about the weather, art, favourite pop groups, sport. Actually anything at all will do since the topic is simply the vehicle for the "getting to know you process."

We normally start by exchanging formal information about ourselves. We learn each other's name, where we are from, what work we do, and so on. Some people find conversation with a stranger rather awkward, and this phase can be punctuated by embarrassing silences. This is the stage when we are walking on eggshells. We are testing the water so to speak and being on our best behaviour. We would not normally express our deepest feelings to an acquaintance. If someone we hardly know asks us the formal question, "How are you?" we give the formal reply, "Fine, thank you." A detailed account of our medical history or our little worries is not wanted at this time. Two things can happen at this stage: we can go our separate ways and never give each other another thought, or the relationship can develop further. The young people may find that they have little in common and so their initial mutual interest will quickly evaporate.

There could be many reasons why some relationships never move beyond the stage of acquaintanceship. It may be shyness, lack of interest, or lack of time, or we may just feel that we have nothing in common. It may be that we meet someone once and never see that person again, or perhaps we may bump into each other regularly but have absolutely nothing in common and so always remain at the acquaintanceship level. We all have relationships like that: there is nothing at all wrong with them but they are not very deep. With someone else we find that something "clicks." We find that we have lots of things in common. It may be a similar sense of humour or similar hobbies, or we may just find the other person interesting and want to learn more about him or her. If this interest is mutual it may lead on to further meetings.

2. *Friendliness*

Let us assume that our young friends hit it off right away and so arrange to meet again very soon. They may have learned quite a bit about each other in their first conversation, but there is so much more to learn. The more they meet and talk, the more relaxed are they in each other's company, the more friendly they become. Boundaries begin to be dismantled as they gradually admit each other into areas of their lives that have previously been clearly marked "private." So we may tend to become more friendly and relaxed the more we meet with another person. We have longer conversations, in which we begin to exchange ideas, thoughts, and concerns. Slowly, step by step, we begin the process of revealing ourselves to each other. This process requires time and loyalty. A lot of subtle testing of each other takes place and no lasting relationship has been made at this point. Many things could cause us to lose touch, such as lack of time or one moving away. We may of course discover that we did not have as much in common as we first thought and either drift away or begin to find excuses not to meet so often.

There may be many reasons why relationships do not develop beyond the point of friendliness. If we are fortunate we may maintain friendly relationships with our neighbours and with various other people we meet throughout our lives. These are not friends in the proper sense of that word but people with whom we can have a fairly relaxed conversation for a few minutes whenever we meet them.

3. *Friendship*

The young couple have met several times now and have begun to share their hopes and dreams. There is a deepening of what has gone before. They begin to experience the truth of the description of friendship attributed to George Eliot: "Oh the comfort, the inexpressible comfort of feeling safe with a person: having neither to weigh thoughts nor measure words but to pour them out. Just as they are—chaff and grain together, knowing that a faithful hand will take and sift them, keep what is worth keeping, and then with the breath of kindness, blow the rest away."

The terms "friend" and "friendship" tend to be used rather loosely to cover a wide range of relationships ranging from the superficial to the intimate. Sometimes we can keep people at a distance: we may call them friends, but they are not permitted really to know us since we will not share our deepest hopes and fears with them. If we really do establish a close friendship we make a commitment to the other person and that person makes a commitment to us. This is not necessarily a public commitment, but both parties know that this is no longer simply a casual relationship from which they can walk away at any time without causing great hurt.

To return to the young couple for a moment: they think often of one another now. They look forward very much to the times when they can be together, because that is when they feel really alive. Friendship puts the sunlight into life. With time, perhaps over years, certainly over some months, a true friendship can develop. It is a growth in intimacy that may or may not have a sexual element, a growth in affection and respect for each other. A friend is a person with whom you dare to be yourself. You no longer have to pretend to be something you are not. You are now accepted by the other as who and what you are.

In time, if we persevere through the normal ups and downs that every relationship undergoes, we can feel more free to disclose more of ourselves, knowing that this self-disclosure will be accepted with understanding and sympathy. A friend is worthy of that name only when he or she accepts us as we are. This acceptance gives a feeling of great confidence as we feel free to speak our own truth and to listen to the truth of someone else. Friends can and do have a great influence on us. They can and do affect our ideas, our views, even our mannerisms. This is the time when commitments are made. A true friendship cannot exist with someone who is afraid of commitment. This is why a crisis can develop at this point as we begin to feel insecure and very vulnerable, or perhaps we come to the realization that we do not want to be committed to this person, or we break off the friendship for fear of being abandoned by the other. There is usually some sort of crisis in a relationship when the couple begin to glimpse some of the implications of loving another person.

When the two young friends first met they kept the conversation flowing because it is important at an early stage in a relationship to find out a great deal about each other. What they discovered formed the basis for their growing friendship and commitment to each other. They struggled through arguments and misunderstandings, through the ups and downs that occur in any relationship. They have begun to discover some of the shadow side of each other and they gradually accept the reality of each other. The well-behaved and well-polished performances they gave on their first few meetings are now replaced by a true encounter of two real human beings. As the relationship grows, they become much more comfortable just being together in a companionable silence.

As friendship develops much talking becomes less necessary and silence begins to develop as a normal way of communicating. Indeed, it is discovered that much more can be communicated through silence than through many words. A relationship of friendship can grow throughout the years to a stage where words become almost superfluous and where silence is filled with meaning.

4. Intimacy
If we continue with the friendship there is the possibility of it developing to ever greater depths. There can be a feeling of

mutual support when either can freely give up their own preferences for the happiness of the other. It is as though they begin to think as one, each knowing what the other likes or dislikes. It is not a taking over of one by the other but more a working in mutual harmony, where if one is happy so is the other and both live to make the other happy. There is great contentment in just being in each other's company. Here silence truly is eloquent.

The young couple have grown older together and grown in their commitment to each other. A long time ago they gave each other permission to "wander the corridors of my heart." They know each other very well, and there is no great need to talk a lot. They love each other, and their love has been tested and tried by the vagaries of life. They want to be in each other's company not to discuss the latest political scandal or even that most interesting of topics, the weather. They simply want to be with each other in love.

It is impossible to describe in detail a friendship that has grown to the level of intimacy because each such relationship will be unique. There are as many levels of intimacy as there are individuals, but no matter how close two people are there always remains some element of mystery. We can never know the other completely because of the essential mystery of the human person. Sometimes we can catch a glimpse of a previously unexpected character trait in a close friend, and this opens up yet another path to be explored.

Chapter Two

GROWING IN PRAYER

Just as one can grow in a human relationship so also is it possible to grow in the relationship with God. We are subject to change but God is not. Wherever we go, God is there waiting for us always ready to forgive, to heal, to take up where we left off. Psalm 139 expresses this truth beautifully:

> O LORD, you have searched me and known me.
> You know when I sit down and when I rise up;
>   you discern my thoughts from far away.
> You search out my path and my lying down,
>   and are acquainted with all my ways.
> Even before a word is on my tongue,
>   O LORD, you know it completely.
> You hem me in, behind and before,
>   and lay your hand upon me.
> Such knowledge is too wonderful for me;
>   it is so high that I cannot attain it.
> Where can I go from your spirit?
>   Or where can I flee from your presence?
> If I ascend to heaven, you are there;
>   if I make my bed in Sheol, you are there.
> If I take the wings of the morning
>   and settle at the farthest limits of the sea,
> even there your hand shall lead me,
>   and your right hand shall hold me fast.
> If I say, "Surely the darkness shall cover me,
>   and the light around me become night,"
> even the darkness is not dark to you;
>   the night is as bright as the day,
>   for darkness is as light to you.
> For it was you who formed my inward parts;
>   you knit me together in my mother's womb.

I praise you, for I am fearfully and wonderfully made.
   Wonderful are your works;
that I know very well.
   My frame was not hidden from you,
when I was being made in secret,
   intricately woven in the depths of the earth.
Your eyes beheld my unformed substance.
In your book were written all the days that
were formed for me,
   when none of them as yet existed.
How weighty to me are your thoughts, O God!
   How vast is the sum of them!
I try to count them—they are more than the sand;
   I come to the end—I am still with you."

(Ps.139:1-18)

The Christian community normally plays an important role in the development of one's relationship with God. The Church is the community of believers in Jesus Christ, and, especially through common worship, we support one another on the spiritual journey. Our personal prayer is nourished by the sacraments and especially in the Eucharist. While in this book we are focussing on the individual's relationship with God, the communal nature of the Christian faith must never be forgotten. We go to God as members of a community, and the acid test of the health of our relationship with God is how we actually treat our neighbours in daily life.

A usual way to begin this relationship consciously is by reciting traditional vocal prayers. Many of these come directly from the word of God, and others have been hallowed by centuries of use by Christians. These may always play an important part in our relationship with God but if they remain the sum total of our prayer life without even any attempt at being aware of whom we are addressing, our prayer runs the risk of being superficial. Prayer must mean more than finding the right words, formula, or ritual.

Some people seem to be under a compulsion to go through routines of prayer and just "get their prayers in." This can occur for many reasons. Perhaps there is simply no one who is able to lead people forward in their faith, or perhaps an individual has no desire to move forward. Words are one way in which human beings communicate but certainly not the only way and perhaps not even the most important way. Words can also be used as a barrier and can prevent the other person from getting too close. Certainly in the relationship with God we need to learn not to act like those who think that by using many words they will make themselves heard by God: we must not be like those people (cf. Matt. 6:7). It is interesting to note some of the different translations of this verse in different versions of the Bible: for example, the NRSV uses "do not heap up empty phrases"; the New American Bible has "In your prayer do not rattle on like the pagans. They think they will win a hearing by the sheer multiplication of words"; the Good News Bible, "When you pray, do not use a lot of meaningless words, as the pagans do, who think that God will hear them because their prayers are long." Vocal prayers, even long ones, have their place, but it must not be thought that the more words we use, the more pleasing we will be to God or the surer we will be of having our prayer answered.

The apostles asked Jesus to teach them how to pray, just as John the Baptist taught his disciples how to pray. These apostles were all good Jews who had been brought up in the tradition of the Psalms and the synagogue worship. They knew how to pray, but they wanted more. They saw something special in Jesus. They sensed that he had a special relationship with God, and they wanted to share in this in some way. Jesus then taught them what we know as the Lord's Prayer. He did not simply teach his friends a specially efficacious form of words; he taught them a way to relate on intimate terms as with one's father. We are not simply creatures of Almighty God; we are children. We have a duty to glorify God's name and to work for the coming of the Kingdom. Therefore we seek God's will in all things rather than our own. We acknowledge our total dependence on God and we recognize also that we are sinners in need of healing. We ask pardon for our offences and make this dependent on our willingness to forgive those who have offended us.

Ideally, prayer should be a normal and natural expression of our relationship with God. Prayer is what makes the relationship with God grow, what keeps it healthy. Indeed we could say that prayer is the relationship with God. Throughout the centuries many ways of prayer have been used by faithful Christians, and we can learn something from all of them. However, those ways that bring the individual into contact with the word of God in the scriptures are the most enduring.

Lectio Divina

It has been said that the most traditional way of growing in the relationship with God is through the ancient practice of lectio divina or praying the scriptures. This was the way of prayer of those who went out alone into the desert in the first Christian centuries and was developed by the early monks who gathered together in communities to support one another. Originally the hermit or monk would learn thePsalms by heart and throughout the day savour the word of God by calling a Psalm to mind while going about his ordinary tasks. The whole of the Bible was a fruitful source for prayer. This way of prayer provided the opportunity for the individual to appropriate the inner meaning of the communal prayer. This way of prayer is once again becoming very popular.[1] There is nothing esoteric about this way of responding to God. In fact it could be said that it is the most natural way of prayer.

21

Prayer could be said to have various levels just like human relationships and for the purposes of this book we want to follow the stages of this prayer called *lectio divina*. A strict translation of the words would give in English "divine reading." It refers to reading the scriptures as the word of God or, perhaps more exactly, praying the scriptures. It seemed to be the natural and normal way of prayer for centuries, and apparently no one thought of systematizing it until Guigo the Carthusian did so in the twelfth century.[2] He laid out four basic steps to this ancient way of prayer:

> Reading *(lectio)* is the careful study of the scriptures, concentrating all one's powers on it. Meditation *(meditatio)* is the busy application of the mind to seek with the help of one's own reason for knowledge of hidden truths. Prayer (oratio) is the heart's devoted turning to God to drive away evil and obtain what is good. Contemplation *(contemplatio)* is when the mind is in some sort lifted up to God and held above itself, so that it tastes the joys of everlasting sweetness.[3]

It is our conviction that these four steps of *lectio* also describe the normal development of a healthy and maturing prayer life. *(i)* *lectio—reading: Lectio* means reading, but not the normal way we read. It is not like scanning the newspapers because of shortage of time; nor glancing at a list of television programmes; nor the way we would read a novel for entertainment; nor the way we would read a textbook because we are studying for an exam or as a purely intellectual pursuit. What kind of reading is *lectio*? It is a kind that does not come naturally to modern men and women. Originally the hermits and monks would read the scriptures aloud and slowly in order to impress the words on their minds. Therefore it is the opposite of our modern speed-reading. It is a slow and reverent reading, which is really a listening to God. It is a way of converting our reading into prayer. This is the word of life for us; it can and will change our life if only we consent. The first stage of this consent is this reverent listening to the word of God in the Bible. We read the scriptures as the word of God addressed to us here and now. If we were to really believe that God was speaking to us through the words of the Bible, we would most certainly treasure the words and read them with the utmost care. *Lectio* is like reading a letter from someone we love.

Many people are taught to pray as children. We learn to say prayers even before we can read. If you were brought up as a Christian you might have learned the traditional scripture-based prayers—the Our Father and the Hail Mary—or you may have been introduced to the Bible early on. So although we may not be actually reading the scriptures at this stage we are brought into contact with them by the words of the prayers. Another way of coming into contact with the word of God is through listening to the scriptures being read in church.

Whichever way we come into contact with the word, we begin to get to know God. The prayers we are taught or the Bible stories we learn tell us something about how God acts. As we have seen, this stage in a human relationship is quite precarious. The relationship can stop there for a variety of reasons, and so can the relationship with God. Some people find talking to someone they do not know rather difficult. How much more difficult it is to go into the presence of someone very important—we can very easily become tongue-tied. God knows what we are made of, and so we have been provided with topics of conversation in the Bible stories or in our formal prayers. These prayers will always remain important for us, but if all we ever do is rush through a few formal prayers without even thinking about their meaning,perhaps our relationship with God is not very deep. With acquaintances we keep the conversation on a formal level; if we stay at this level it is very superficial. We are invited to move deeper, to get closer to God. Of course we do not

23

think, "Now I am ready to move on to stage 2." It is a normal, natural, almost effortless flow. The reverent reading or listening leads us to want to get to know God a little better. *(ii) Meditatio—meditation or reflecting:* The actual word Guigo used to describe the second step of *lectio divina* is *meditatio*—meditation. This is a word that has come to have many meanings, but in its most original Christian sense it referred to the method the early monastics used to memorize the Psalms and other passages of scripture in order to grasp the meaning of the text, which then acted as a springboard for contemplative prayer.[4] From this beginning it came to mean reflection on scripture or on the things of God, and this is the meaning that will be employed throughout this work. So most people who pray will actually have done some form of meditation whether they realize it or not, because it simply means reflecting on God or the things of God. This is a stage of growth in the relationship with God—not that we ever leave the first stage of reading or listening behind—in which we are now willing to take God seriously and to seek to apply God's word to our own lives. Meditation, then, is when you reflect on the prayers you say or the words you read in scripture. This means that God is becoming quite important in your life; you are beginning to spend time in God's presence, thinking over God's ways and words. At this time, you have moved beyond the acquaintanceship stage with God, but it is still not a deep relationship. If we consent, the word of God will move beyond our minds and penetrate our hearts. Then we really begin to pray from the heart.

The second step of the *lectio divina* way of prayer is reflecting on the word of God. The ancient monks would memorize the Psalms and other parts of scripture so that when they were working at their daily tasks they could bring the word of God to mind and reflect on it whenever their minds were not fully occupied on other tasks. An image that can be used for this activity is a cow chewing the cud. We need to chew on the scriptures, as it were, in order to extract from them everything the Lord wants to give us. When we learned to say our prayers we might well also have been taught to try to think about the meaning of the words we were using and to think about the God we were speaking to. Gradually, as we grew from childhood to adulthood we might have been taught to say our prayers quietly and think more about the words. In all these forms of prayer we commune with God through the use of words, images, feelings, gestures, signs, symbols, and thoughts. This is an excellent formation for the personal relationship with God and is itself prayer. It is a kind of prayer we never grow out of and never leave, no matter how sophisticated we may become.

Over a period of time, if we continue to be faithful, we tend to become more friendly and relaxed in God's company. The conversation becomes less formal and we begin to share with God some of our own thoughts and ideas. We are not just telling God what we want but sharing something of ourselves. Like a human relationship this stage takes time to develop. If we do not keep in touch with God regularly the relationship can easily stagnate.

(iii) *Oratio—prayer:* At some point in a developing relationship with God what we say to God and what we think about God penetrate the heart, and we begin to respond to God not merely with the lips or with our thoughts but from the depths of our being. This is the third step of *lectio divina*, where we pray from the heart. In the sixth century St Benedict, the inspiration of modern monasticism, "conceived of prayer not as the saying of prayers or singing of psalms, but as a relatively short period of silent intimate address to God, the fruit of the practice of *lectio/meditatio* that was institutionalized in the monastery as a silent pause after each psalm in the Divine Office."[5]

It is not possible to say what will arise from our hearts when we are in conversation with God because, like any conversation, it has a life of its own. Perhaps it will be an expression of sorrow or praise or thanksgiving or some other emotion which wells up from deep in our hearts. This involves a qualitative shift in the relationship with God. It is no longer a hit-and-miss affair, but God now becomes very important to us. We want to spend time with God; perhaps it may feel like a dam bursting, or perhaps it will be a quieter experience. However it happens, we begin to pray spontaneously. While we continue to use traditional prayers, we now also want to use our own words to express our feelings toward God.

The Charismatic Movement has been a great help to very many people in encouraging them to use their emotions in prayer. For the first time many felt free to be themselves before God and to express what was in their hearts. The charismatic way of prayer does not suit everyone, of course, but we are all called to relate to God as we are, and therefore the spontaneous prayer that arises from our hearts in whatever form is important in the growing relationship with God.

This is the time when a true friendship with God begins to develop. Just as in a human relationship, there is often some sort of crisis at this stage. The crisis can take many forms, but often prayer becomes very dry just as we are getting used to a greater ease in conversing with God and enjoying emotional satisfaction in the relationship. We can search for ways that might give us that satisfaction again, and when we fail to find them we may give up prayer in the sense of searching for God and settle for saying the occasional formal prayer. Why should we make the effort if God seems to have moved and not left a forwarding address?

If we persevere through this we begin to accept God on God's terms and not on our terms. We learn that we cannot turn God on and off like the hot water tap. If we continue walking with God at God's pace, gradually the amount of words we use when talking to God will reduce; our prayer will naturally simplify over a period of time. This third stage of *lectio*, which traditionally has been called *oratio*, is intended to flow naturally into the fourth stage.

(iv)   Contemplatio—contemplation: There comes a time when we need to lay aside our own ideas, thoughts, words, images, and the like because they can no longer express what is in the heart. The heart is too full to speak. Silent prayer is a normal development of prayer and should not be thought to be unusual, because at times silence is the only adequate human response to God. Most people have experienced a moment when human words and thoughts are not enough and when silence is the most appropriate response. Have you ever been stunned into silence by a beautiful sunset? Have you ever held a new-born baby in your arms? Have you ever experienced an emotion that was too deep for words? This experience is quite normal and is a normal stage of a developing relationship with God. Guigo the Carthusian called the fourth stage of the *lectio divina* process *contemplatio*, contemplation.

All prayer is a response to the grace of God, but until we come to this point it is also very much our effort. What we do can range from reading the scriptures over and over again to thinking about a gospel passage or even just directing one word of love to God; it is still our effort. The point about contemplation is that no effort is involved. This is where God takes over. St John of the Cross says that contemplation is nothing other than a secret, peaceful, and loving inflow of God, which, if not hampered, inflames the soul in the spirit of love.[6] What does that mean? It is impossible to explain because the experience goes beyond our human boundaries. There are no words to describe the experience of God flowing into one's very being. Even the word "experience" is inadequate, because it is not something we can feel or see or hear in the normal sense of those terms, nor is it like anything we have ever experienced before. For this reason St John of the Cross often equates contemplation with darkness, because our normal ways of knowing become inadequate and we must learn a new way of knowing, which can be taught by God alone.

The tradition tells us that normally God leads us by grace to repentance and to amendment of life. We then begin to seek the face of God in meditation. As St John of the Cross says: "Seek in reading and you will find in meditation; knock in prayer and it will be opened to you in contemplation."[7] However, God is not bound by rules. God can and very often does act completely outside the rules. So it may be that God will reach up and pull the individual down, as it were to experience a moment of contemplation without any previous effort on the person's part. This is like a push-start to get us going on the journey. It is as if God were saying, "You think that was good. Well, you ain't seen nothing yet!"

Unfortunately we can easily misunderstand the experience or not follow up on it, but God never gives up and will approach us in many different ways until finally we hear and respond.

However, the normal process seems to be that our prayer becomes simpler with fewer words. Letting go of our own effort, our own words and concepts, seems to reduce the barriers to this peaceful and loving inflow of God. At the beginning, contemplation is hidden because it is so gentle or because we are covered in darkness and confusion. The last thing we think we are experiencing is the peaceful and loving inflow of God, but gradually our false self is put to death and we begin, painfully slowly at first, to see with the eyes of God. We begin to see God in the nothingness and hear God's voice in the silence.

However, if we remember that silence is a normal way to communicate in a close relationship, perhaps we will not worry so much when our prayer tends toward silence. For a while we may regret the passing of emotional highs when we pray, and we may fear that we are going backwards or perhaps that God has forgotten about us or has rejected us. If we truly desire God and are doing our best to do God's will, the more likely explanation for our confusion is that our relationship with God is changing to a point where we do not need so many words and where God communicates with us in another way. Again St John of the Cross counsels that what is most necessary in order to make progress is to keep silent before this great God with our desires and our tongue, because the language God best hears is silent love.[8]

Contemplation is pure gift. There is nothing we can do to earn it or make it happen. This is the point when many good Christians stop. Instinctively we may feel that this is too high for us, that contemplation is fine for monks and nuns but is not for the likes of you or me. This is the tragic result of various historical problems, as a consequence of which suspicion was cast on the idea of contemplation and on those who aspired to it. For the past four hundred years contemplation—unfortunately—tended to be reserved for an élite group within the Church, for the spiritual equivalent of Olympic athletes. It was not thought at all suitable for "ordinary people." Now contemplation is more and more understood as the normal flowering of a mature Christian life, begun in baptism, by means of which we are immersed in the life of God. We do not earn the gift of contemplation because of our outstanding holiness. It is not the reward for a holy life; it is a necessity for a truly holy life. The acid test of holiness of course is how one lives in daily life—the constancy of one's love.

Contemplation is the gift of God and is not something we can grasp hold of or conjure up by using any clever technique. It has been called "resting in God" beyond words, thoughts and images.[9] This is God's gift, and although we cannot make this happen we can prepare ourselves to receive the gift. It is rather like wanting to catch a bus. The best way to catch this bus is to stand at the right stop. We cannot complain that our bus never comes or does not stop if we are standing somewhere else. So we can prepare ourselves to receive this gift by developing our relationship with God to an extent that we are quite comfortable with silence. In silence we learn to listen to the still small voice of God. To quote St John of the Cross again:

> One word the Father spoke,
> which word was His Son,
> and this word He speaks
> ever in eternal silence,
> and in silence must it
> be heard by the soul."[10]

There is a time to read, a time to pray vocally, and a time to ponder. In a maturing prayer-life all of these will at some time no longer give the satisfaction they once did. This is a time of crisis, especially for those who do not know that this is quite normal and to be expected. It does not mean that we are lukewarm but paradoxically is a wonderful sign of growth in our relationship with God. The great temptation is to run away from the engulfing silence and to fill the emptiness with many things. The essential is for us simply to wait in the silence. God is busy creating a masterpiece, and we must be careful lest we get in the way. Most of us will need some help simply to wait in the silence for God. The tendency is for our minds to wander all over the place, and we often feel that our prayer-time has been a constant battle against distractions. For those who feel the need of a help, a practice such as Centering Prayer offers it. Centering Prayer is not a magical technique, nor should it replace any of our other ways of prayer. It is a very simple way of letting go of our own agenda so that we can consent to God's will.

Centering Prayer is not part of the *lectio divina* way of prayer but is closely related to it in that Centering Prayer seeks to facilitate the movement from simple spontaneous prayer to a silent prayer in which we simply consent to God's presence and action. In silence, then, we await God's gift of contemplation.

Where does Centering Prayer fit into the structure of *lectio*? Centering Prayer is a method of prayer based on the fourteenth-century English spiritual classic, *The Cloud of Unknowing*[11] and the insights of some of the great writers of the Christian contemplative tradition. It is also modern in the sense that it addresses a modern problem. We are very analytical; we have to use our minds to tease out the problems of life. We are used to living in our heads. When it comes to prayer we do not change our basic approach to life and so we find it very hard to let go of our own ideas and thoughts. This letting-go is very difficult for us as we are very active people. There is also the fact that suspicion was once cast (by the Inquisition) on the contemplative call, that is the call to intimacy with God that lies at the heart of every Christian vocation, but it was never completely extinguished: people continued to respond to God's call to intimacy. We have probably all from time to time met people who are clearly very far advanced on the spiritual journey, but there have been times when there was no encouragement to seek the gift of contemplation—indeed the opposite was the case: contemplation was for the élite in the Church. But how common was it even among the so-called élite? Now we are becoming aware once again that contemplation is for all.

So, Centering Prayer is a human method of prayer that reduces the obstacles to contemplation by helping us to let go of our own thoughts and allow space for God to act. It is not contemplation. Prayer is what we do; contemplation is what God does.

31

Chapter Three

THE METHOD OF CENTERING PRAYER

If prayer really is a relationship with God, why on earth do we need methods of prayer? Surely this complicates what should be utterly simple? If you find that human relationships present no problems to you, then enjoy your desert island! The rest of the human race knows very well how much skill is involved in relating to someone else. Most of these necessary skills are picked up unconsciously through our education and home environment: it is very difficult to teach someone later in life the little social skills that make life in common bearable. Just as we need certain skills in human relationships, so also there are certain things to be learned regarding how to relate to God. Of course every time we pray we use some method of prayer. This may be a method hallowed by tradition, or it may be a method thought up by oneself. It may be very complex or quite simple, long or short. It may be a series of prayers we say regularly, or meditation on some scene from the Gospels, or talking to God about the events of one's day, or a way to focus the mind in order to avoid distractions, or simply trying to be still in the presence of the One whom we know loves us.

As the previous chapter has shown, *lectio divina* is the most traditional way of cultivating friendship with Christ. Through the scriptures, God speaks to us and we have ready-made topics of conversation. It is important to have topics for conversation at the beginning of a relationship because silence can be acutely embarrassing. As we talk to God we will be drawn to reflect on the great truths of faith. This reflection will help us to become aware of what God has done for us and will, we hope, touch our hearts. When we respond from the heart to God's word we are entering an intimate relationship with God. There are various difficulties we can encounter on the road to intimacy, difficulties that can prevent us from continuing the journey or at least make it difficult for us to progress very far. The wisdom of the Christian tradition has given us several ways or methods to help us on our journey. If we really want to respond to God's invitation to intimacy, if we really want to move beyond our own activity simply to rest in God, we shall certainly need some help, because human beings do not find it easy to abandon control.

The method of Centering Prayer is a way we believe can help us "let go and let God." We are certainly not suggesting that it is the best or the only way of prayer; we simply want to share it because we have found it helpful in our own lives and we have seen its effects in the lives of many others.

Before describing what Centering Prayer is, it may be helpful to say what it is not. First of all, in the method of Centering Prayer we are not trying to make our minds a blank. The effort to do that, if it is successful, ends up with— surprise, surprise—an empty mind. As Thomas Merton wrote, "An emptiness that is deliberately cultivated, for the sake of fulfilling a personal spiritual ambition, is not empty at all: it is full of itself. It is so full that the light of God cannot get into it anywhere . . ."[12] Centering Prayer is not a relaxation exercise. Some people who practise Centering Prayer do find it relaxing for a time, but that is certainly not the purpose. The purpose is to open ourselves completely to the presence and purifying action of God, which is not usually described as relaxing. Centering Prayer is not a technique in that it does not pretend to provide an easy path to holiness. There is absolutely no promise attached, such as "If you do this twice a day, you will become a saint." It does not involve the use of a mantra as used in Eastern forms of meditation and Transcendental Meditation. Mantric prayer is a prayer of attention in that the mantra helps to focus the mind on God. Centering Prayer is a prayer of intention that focuses the heart on God.

33

Centering Prayer is not intended to replace any of our other ways of prayer but can enhance them all. It is not contemplative prayer but is an aid to open us to the depths of contemplative prayer. It is a very simple way of letting go of our own agenda so that we can consent to God's will. To consent to God's will is to consent to be transformed by the purifying action of God. All prayer must eventually lead to this consent: "Thy will be done."

Centering Prayer has its roots in the tradition of contemplative prayer that has existed within the Church since earliest times and, in particular, is based on the teaching contained in *The Cloud of Unknowing*.[13] Pope St Gregory the Great at the end of the sixth century used a wealth of images to describe contemplation. The terms "love," "desire," "seeking," "knowledge," "vision," "contemplation" all imply each other and are often used by him almost interchangeably. For Gregory, contemplation is a knowledge through love, and it was he who coined the famous phrase "love itself is a form of knowledge."[14] For him, contemplation was both the fruit of reflecting on the word of God in scripture and also at the same time a precious gift of God. He called this "resting in God." In this "resting" the mind and heart are not so much seeking God as beginning to experience, to "taste" God whom they have been seeking. This is not a state of suspension of all activity but the reduction of many acts and reflections to a single act or thought to sustain one's consent to God's presence and action.

Centering Prayer is both a relationship and a discipline. Any relationship requires time and effort if it is to grow and mature. If we do not give time to prayer we cannot expect it to deepen. Centering Prayer is a discipline in that it provides a method to help one to be still and to listen to God in the silence. The method of Centering Prayer is very simple, so simple that its very effortlessness can make some people think they are doing nothing but wasting time. Yet in persevering with this way one soon discovers that it is very hard work indeed. There are a number of methods designed to facilitate the gift of contemplative prayer. We make no claim here that Centering Prayer is better than any other method, but we do stress the importance of getting the recipe right, as it were. A really good meringue needs an added sprinkling of sugar just before replacing it in the oven for its final five minutes. Imagine the taste if one added salt instead of sugar! Salt and sugar may look the same at a cursory glance, but they certainly do not have the same effect. Therefore it is important to stick to the method if one wants to use Centering Prayer— or indeed any other method of prayer.

To prepare for a period of Centering Prayer, pick a time when you are not overtired, because to fall asleep is not the purpose of the prayer—though it may happen! Try to find a quiet place where you will not normally be interrupted. This too might seem a rather difficult suggestion for those who do not have the luxury of a nearby chapel, or whose children always seem to demand attention just at the time for prayer. We need to be creative to find a time and a place where disturbances will be at a minimum. As the Gospel says, the one who searches always finds! We are ingenious at finding time for anything we really want to do. If prayer is a priority for us, we will find the time in the midst of the busiest schedule.

Centering Prayer reduces the tendency to be over-active in prayer and to depend excessively on human concepts in order to reach God, who is beyond all concepts. Its purpose is not to induce some altered state of consciousness but simply to reduce the obstacles in us that prevent us from following the delicate inspirations of the Holy Spirit. All that Centering Prayer requires of us is that we keep a loving intention to be in God's presence and to consent to God's action in our lives. We do this by using a simple word of our own choosing to draw our intention gently back to God whenever we become aware of any kind of distraction. We need do nothing more; we simply trust that God will accept our intention and make it bear fruit.

Centering Prayer is not saying prayers; nor is it an intellectual meditation on a scriptural text, though these are valuable spiritual exercises that can have their place in our normal devotions. Centering Prayer is intended to complement and complete them but not replace them.

There are four simple guidelines to the method of Centering Prayer. These are:

1. Choose a sacred word as the symbol of your intention to consent to the presence and action of God within;

2. Sitting comfortably and with eyes closed, settle briefly and silently introduce the sacred word as the symbol of your intention to consent to God's presence and action;

3. When you become aware of thoughts, return ever so gently to the sacred word;

4. At the end of the prayer period, remain in silence for a few minutes with eyes closed.

Let us examine each of these guidelines in greater detail.

1. Choose a sacred word as the symbol of your intention to consent to the presence and action of God within.

In the method of Centering Prayer, the term "sacred word" is a technical term. It does not necessarily mean a holy word. The sacred word is sacred not because of its inherent meaning but because of your intention. The sacred word could actually be anything so long as it is sacred *for you.* Most people seem to choose a name for God, such as "Lord," "Jesus," "Spirit," "Father," "Abba"; others choose a word that symbolizes the interior movement, such as "Peace," "Love," "Calm," "Silence," or the like; or it could be a neutral word, such as "Mercy," "Faith," "Trust." The author of *The Cloud of Unknowing* says, "If you want this intention summed up in a word, to retain it more easily, take a short word, preferably of one syllable, to do so. The shorter the word the better being more like the working of the Spirit. A word like 'God' or 'Love'. Choose which you like, or perhaps some other, so long as it is of one syllable. And fix this word fast to your heart, so that it is always there come what may."[15]

It is important to point out early on that the sacred word is *not* a mantra. "Mantra" is a term that has come from the Eastern religions and often seems to be used in the West without a great deal of understanding. Traditionally the mantra is chosen by the guru and handed down to the disciple; its importance lies in its sound and its constant repetition, which is intended to bring the user to an altered state of consciousness. We are not here criticizing the use of the mantra in Christian prayer but simply trying to get the recipe right, as it were, or to make sure that we are using one method of prayer and not our own peculiar mixture.

So what is a sacred word? It is the symbol of our intention to consent to God's presence and action in our lives. A symbol represents a deeper reality. Take for example the symbol of the wedding ring. It is not just a band of more or less expensive metal. It represents the love of the couple. For some, unfortunately, the same symbol can represent a shackle. The meaning depends very much on what the individual puts on it. Think also of the wedding ceremony: the woman and the man are asked individually to commit themselves to each other. To the questions, they reply "I do." These little words are of very great importance. They are intended to convey the love and commitment of one human being for and to another. These same words can be used in very different circumstances to mean something completely different. On a very hot day someone might ask you, "Do you like ice cream?" Your reply, "I do!" might be heartfelt at the time but surely it does not have the same importance as the words of the bride and groom. The same words are used with very different meanings.

So the sacred word can be a very simple word, but if it is your symbol of your intention to consent to God's presence and action, then it is truly sacred. It is a good idea to spend some time thinking about which sacred word to use. Perhaps you could put this book down and give it some thought now. You may want to ask the Holy Spirit for guidance or perhaps a word rises naturally within you as the fruit of your ongoing prayer life. Whatever word you choose, let it be for you a symbol of your desire to surrender your whole being to God. The brief word can speak volumes when it sums up everything you want to say to God.

Once we have chosen a sacred word, we do not change it during the prayer period because that would be to start thinking again. Some people like to experiment by changing the sacred word every so often. Ideally one should choose a word and stick with it. Use of the same word over a lengthy period of time allows it to sink deep within us and it can then act as a trigger whenever we go to prayer.

The sacred word is the symbol of one's intention to consent to the presence and action of God within. Centering Prayer is a prayer of intention not attention: we do not focus our minds on any particular object during the time of prayer. The important thing is that our will consent to God's presence and action. If the will does consent it does not matter that the imagination is running around like an unruly child. Of course it is uncomfortable and annoying when we are filled with distractions, but the important thing is for the will to consent. This means that I may be sitting under an avalanche of distractions but want to be in God's presence whatever that may feel like, and I want to say "yes" to God's action whatever that may mean for my life.

The intention is absolutely crucial because it is the intention to consent to God's presence and action within that makes the prayer. Without that intention it is not prayer but could be simply a relaxation exercise. Switching off from our busy lives for twenty minutes could be a relaxing experience and might even be therapeutic. However, if our intention is not to relax but to consent to God's presence and action, this becomes a very powerful prayer. What we feel when we pray is not so important as long as our intention to consent to the presence and action of God is firm.

We may imagine that being in God's presence is lovely and peaceful, but we have to remember that we also consent to God's action. The Christian contemplative tradition speaks of the purifying action of God. We need to be purified not only from actual sin but also from anything opposed to God in our lives. If we are to become a vessel of God's presence in our world we need to be hollowed out, as it were, to make space for God. Usually we are so full of ourselves that we have no room for God or anyone else. The action of God then is to purify us of selfishness so that we can become filled with God.[16]

Some people may find the use of a sacred word a problem. In that case a simple inward gaze upon God may be preferred. This is not a picture in the imagination but a gaze of faith on God who is present within. It is used in exactly the same way as the sacred word. Whenever one becomes aware of thoughts, one ever so gently returns to gaze upon God within as the symbol of one's intention to consent to the presence and action of God.

2. Sitting comfortably and with eyes closed, settle briefly and silently introduce the sacred word as the symbol of your intention to consent to God's presence and action.

This is intended as a very practical guideline. Whenever we try to sit still we very shortly become aware of little discomforts. These small aches and pains can be quite distracting and so it is advisable to settle down in a comfortable position that we can easily maintain for the whole period of prayer. This is simply a guideline and there can be no hard and fast rules as to what position is or is not comfortable.

So by "sitting comfortably" we mean relatively comfortably, not so comfortable that we encourage sleep but comfortable enough to avoid thinking about the discomfort of our bodies during the time of prayer. One can pray in any position, of course, but some positions are more conducive to longer periods of sitting still than others. It is recommended that a minimum time for Centering Prayer is twenty minutes. While kneeling is a traditional position for prayer, it is difficult to maintain this position without being distracted from time to time by discomfort. Also if we learn to pray while sitting down, we can pray anywhere—in a bus, train, or plane without being obvious.

It is usually found to be most comfortable to sit with the back straight and well supported by the chair. The head should be free and both feet placed firmly on the floor. The hands can be left free or perhaps placed in one's lap. There is nothing esoteric or mysterious about this position. It is simply what has been found by experience as most conducive to prayer for the majority of people.

It is recommended that the eyes are closed as a way of letting go of what is going on around us. When we close our eyes we immediately cut out much of our distractions. It is also suggested that you settle briefly before the prayer begins. A short scripture reading may be helpful to dispose the mind for prayer. The reading is not meant to start thoughts flowing but simply to be a sort of porch to the prayer itself. It is very difficult to move quickly from great activity to silence, and it is useful to have some way of reminding oneself that there is a change of pace and of activity. The porch or the hallway is where we take off our coats and wipe our shoes before entering the living room. The short scripture reading can act as the metaphorical porch reminding the psyche that we are about to pray.

After the brief period of settling we silently introduce our sacred word. This is done inwardly and not with our lips. We do not say the word mentally but simply let it float into our consciousness. The introduction of the sacred word is as gentle as laying a feather on cotton wool. There is no force in this gentlest of activity. The sacred word is not a battering ram or a mantra but simply the symbol of our intention to consent to the presence and action of God within. During the course of the prayer period the sacred word may become vague or even disappear. It is only used when necessary and so can easily drift away from our consciousness.

3. *When you become aware of thoughts, return ever so gently to the sacred word.*

The term "thoughts" in this method is an umbrella term for every perception including sense perceptions, feelings, images, memories, reflections, and commentaries. We examine this idea more thoroughly in the following chapter. Thoughts are an inevitable and normal part of Centering Prayer. The key word in this guideline is "aware." When we are not aware of thoughts going on in our minds, can we be said to have changed our initial intention, symbolized by the sacred word, to be in God's presence and to consent to God's action? As soon as we become aware, we can then make a decision whether to follow the particular thought, whatever it may be, or to return to be in God's presence. We symbolize this desire to return to God by the use of the sacred word. It is as if we were in the middle of a conversation with someone and suddenly something distracted us. We would probably apologize and turn back to the person who was talking to us. The sacred word does this for us and more.

By returning ever so gently to the sacred word, a minimum of effort is indicated. This is the only activity that is initiated by us during the time of Centering Prayer.

4. *At the end of the prayer period, remain in silence for a few minutes with eyes closed*

This guideline, like the second one, is essentially of a practical nature. The reason for this guideline is to give the one who is praying time to become aware of the physical surroundings once again, and it helps to bring the atmosphere of silence into daily life.

There are several ways to indicate the end of the prayer period. If you are a member of a prayer group, one of the members can mark the end of the prayer period by slowly reciting the Our Father while the others listen. If you are on your own, you could use a timer of some sort so long as it is not too loud. Timers on cookers can be quite useful. Some people make a tape with gentle music at the beginning followed by twenty minutes silence and then more gentle music. A radio alarm can be primed to switch on the radio or a cassette after an appropriate time. Usually with practice you get to know your own time and you might not need any aid to mark the end of the period of prayer.

Chapter Four

THE USE OF THE SACRED WORD

When we pray most of us find that we are battling with thoughts all the time. As soon as we settle down into a time of quiet prayer, all sorts of thoughts seem to pop into our minds. It is unrealistic to think that we are ever going to reach a time when we have no thoughts. That is not an aim of Centering Prayer. Neither do we try to make our minds a blank. That is not prayer. What we are trying to do is simply consent to the presence and action of God in our lives. As we have said before, Centering Prayer is a prayer of intention, not attention. We are not focusing our minds on any particular object, and so there is a natural tendency for the mind to wander. There will never be a time in the prayer when we have no thoughts; we may have a period when we are unaware of thoughts. It is our attitude during the period of Centering Prayer that is important; it may best be expressed as "letting go of thoughts." Whenever we think, we think of something, which means that we try to grasp that "something" with a thought. During Centering Prayer we are trying to open ourselves wide to God's love. We do not try to grasp even the thought of God's love. An attitude of letting go means not grasping. The sacred word is a thought intended to dissolve other thoughts. It is a tiny word of immense significance because it symbolizes for us our intention to consent to the presence and action of God.

The term "thoughts" covers every kind of perception. It ranges from what we would all recognize as distractions to the more subtle kind of thoughts that many people would count as a great blessing. In the method of Centering Prayer, whenever we become aware of thoughts, whatever they may be, we simply return ever so gently to the sacred word and let the thought go.

Perhaps it would be helpful to look at different kinds of thoughts and see how each type can be dealt with in the same way.

Ordinary Wanderings of the Imagination

First we have the ordinary wanderings of the imagination or memory. This kind of thought may consist of the things we were doing or thinking about prior to the time of prayer, or it may be some outside noise. Whenever we try to be silent, background noises have a habit of coming to the foreground. Suddenly we become very aware of things that were unnoticed before. If you have ever been part of a group that is supposed to be silent, you will know that every little sound seems to be magnified. You can hear people cough, sneeze, shuffle, cross and uncross their legs, search their handbags, and so on. These commonplace sounds usually do not register until silence falls. If you are not in a group, you may have found the ideal quiet place to pray, but just as you settle down to be alone with God someone starts up a very noisy lawnmower or turns on pop music on the radio. Even the birds seem to conspire against your time of silent prayer by turning up the volume of their singing. In many modern supermarkets the shoppers are greeted with piped music. This music does not distract you from the actual task in hand unless you are suddenly struck by a particular piece, which may be a reminder of a wonderful holiday or even of an old flame. You then find yourself daydreaming in the middle of the aisles; very soon a queue of trolleys builds up around you, and you are unceremoniously pushed out of your reverie. So during Centering Prayer treat the ordinary thoughts and noises as background music.

Do not try to shut these thoughts and noises out of your mind with a great effort; do not even battle against them, because that would be to give them an importance they do not deserve. In any case you cannot shut these noises and thoughts out of your consciousness. They are going to buzz around you whatever you do. In the method of Centering Prayer we advise you simply to let these thoughts come and let them go. If you find that you latch onto anything in particular, simply return ever so gently to the sacred word as the symbol of your intention to consent to the presence and action of God. These ordinary thoughts can be going on all around you, but you do not have to follow them. The sacred word is used only if you have followed a particular thought and you wish to reinstate your intention to be in God's presence.

Attractive Thoughts
Next come what can be described as attractive thoughts. This kind of thought has emotional overtones and presses a button for us. Sometimes we can be rather like a computer, which carries out particular function when certain keys are touched. These attractive thoughts touch keys in our internal computer, and immediately into our minds comes a whole series of other thoughts. Depending on whether the thought is pleasant or unpleasant, we feel a spontaneous like or dislike. This thought may perhaps be of our favourite TV star who sets our heart fluttering, or it could be of our annual tax return, which makes us recoil in horror. Whatever the thought may be, as soon as you become aware that you are thinking of it, return ever so gently to the sacred word.

Insights
Then we can have insights and psychological breakthroughs, which can often occur when we begin to quieten down and perhaps enjoy some peace. Various thoughts can pop into our consciousness regarding the spiritual journey or the nature of

God, or even some insight into our present behaviour. It may be that a priest has to write a sermon for Trinity Sunday and has left it rather late to prepare. So on the Saturday as he prays he may suddenly in a flash understand the mystery of the Trinity. Naturally he will want to jot this down in order to remember it because he will be able to write a book and become famous if in fact he has understood this great mystery. Sadly he very soon discovers that his brilliant idea vanishes like the dew on a sunny day. He has been pulled out of his prayer for nothing. He has started to think, which is a very laudable thing for a priest to do, but there is a time for everything, and the period of Centering Prayer is a time given over to God and not to our own thoughts.

Perhaps instead of solving the mystery of the Trinity, the thought may be a little more mundane—something about one's own psychological make up, for example. We may all of a sudden realize why we become upset in certain situations, or why we do not like a particular individual. It would be very natural to want to think about this insight and to work it into our present understanding of ourselves. However there is a time for that; the time we have decided to dedicate to Centering Prayer is sacred, so we simply return to the sacred word and let go of the fascinating thought. It can easily be taken up outside the time of prayer, and we may well discover that the blinding insight we had during the time of prayer appears very ordinary when we look at it later.

We need a very intimate kind of self-denial in this kind of prayer. It involves the denial of what we are most attached to—our own inmost thoughts and feelings and the source from which they come—the false self.

What should I do if a lovely picture of Jesus comes into my mind during the time of Centering Prayer? Should I not think about Jesus or talk to him—because surely this is an inspiration from God? What if I am inspired to pray for someone? Thinking about Jesus, talking to him, or praying for the needs of another person are all excellent in themselves, and we should spend time doing these things, but we need to remember that we cannot capture and put God in the straitjacket of our thoughts, ideas, and feelings. Any feeling of God's presence, no matter how wonderful it may seem to be, is most certainly not God. It may or may not come from God, so the best way of dealing with it is to let it come and let it go. If I try to hold on to it, I am turning away from God and focusing on my experience instead. The essence of Centering Prayer is to let go of all my own thoughts, ideas, words, images, no matter how holy these may seem to be, and simply rest in the presence of God consenting in faith to God's will for us. There is plenty of time for thinking, talking, and intercession throughout the rest of the day; the time we set aside for Centering Prayer is not for doing but for being, for consenting to the presence and action of God—which consent is symbolized by returning ever so gently to the sacred word whenever we feel that we have changed our intention.

Self-Reflection

A fourth kind of troublesome thought is something we might call self-reflection. This is like taking a step backward from the experience itself. Some people love to watch the sunset, and others take photographs of it. There is nothing wrong with taking a photograph of something beautiful, but it may mean foregoing the actual experience. Sometimes we want to hold on to some experience and keep it forever. However, it is in the nature of experiences to pass. It is very good to reflect on our experiences at some later stage, but during the period we have decided to dedicate to Centering Prayer we let these experiences come and let them go. The presence of God is like the air we breathe. We can have all we want as long as we do not try to possess and hold on to it. We all need air to breathe, so it would seem sensible to put some away for a rainy day, but of course we cannot do this and there is (and always will be, we hope) enough air for everyone. The self-reflective thought may go something like this: "At last I'm getting somewhere," or "I wonder how I managed to get this peace," or perhaps "I can't do this." Whenever you become aware that you are reflecting on your own experience simply return ever so gently to the sacred word.

Unloading of the Unconscious

The final kind of thought we should like to mention here has been called "Unloading of the Unconscious." We live in a very noisy world. Many of us surround ourselves with noise— talking, thinking, radio, TV, and so on. Even when we have exterior silence there can still be a great deal of noise going on inside us, such as interior commentaries on things that happen and people we meet, planning ahead, interior arguments with someone, and so on. Therefore we are not at all used to real silence. When we actually enter a period of silence, our unconscious may take the opportunity of bringing to our attention certain things that we could not give our attention to earlier because of all the noise in our lives. These could be emotions or memories suppressed for some reason. They may arise with a certain amount of energy and urgency. We are not usually aware of where these thoughts come from. At times they can seem to be just a jumble of thoughts or a vague sense of unease.

We learn to live with anxiety and tension, and we develop various forms of defence mechanisms to cope with life. Ordinary rest does not get rid of the tension, but in the deep interior silence that Centering Prayer can bring about the emotional blocks within us can begin slowly to soften. When this softening process is going on, the debris will come to the surface of our consciousness in times when we allow the silence to make a sufficient space in the noise of everyday life. Sometimes insights into the darker side of our personality will emerge during the prayer. We can begin to see below the surface of our actions and come face to face with our real motivation. Our good intentions can begin to look very shabby to us, and we realize that we are not as generous as we once thought.

Self-knowledge is essential for the spiritual journey because it is the basis for humility. According to St Teresa of Avila, humility is the foundation of the spiritual edifice, and God will not build much without that foundation.[17] She described humility as walking in the truth.[18] However, the truth can be rather difficult to accept, and so we may prefer to live with illusion. God will not allow us to deceive ourselves for long if we are truly open. Gradually our true motivation will be revealed to us. If we desire to stand in the truth, we will be given an insight into the emotional needs and demands that percolate inside us, influencing our thinking, feeling, and activity without us being fully aware of them. This can be a painful and discouraging moment. Imagine that you have spent a long time polishing and cleaning a room until it looks spotless: then a battery of high powered lights is brought in to the room, and when they are switched on everything looks very dirty. The room has not suddenly become dirty again. It is just that you were not aware of the extent of the dirt before the powerful lights were turned on. You may very well prefer not to look at the room with the aid of the powerful lights. That is your choice, but if you want to grow in your relationship with God you must be prepared for your illusions about yourself to be revealed in order that they may be cast aside.

If these troublesome thoughts begin to emerge during prayer, do not panic! All you have to do is return ever so gently to the sacred word whenever you become aware that one of these thoughts has engaged you, because the sacred word is your symbol of your intention to consent to God's presence and action in your life. The rising of these thoughts is like God's spring-cleaning of our interior. When God cleans, the house is really clean. This sort of experience can feel very negative, but it can actually be a very positive sign that God is at work in our lives. Therefore be thankful and submit to God's ministrations by consenting to the divine purifying action.

The Centering Prayer method helps to identify the false self, which is the defensive mechanism we have built up over a lifetime. The false self comes about because of our experience of the world, how we were treated and how we coped, our reaction to change, our feelings of insecurity, and our loss of self-worth. We blissfully imagine that we do good from the best of motives, but when this dynamism begins to operate in us we begin to perceive that we are not as generous as we once believed. This is a very uncomfortable feeling, but this transformation process brings with it self-knowledge, and it is only through self-knowledge that we can discover our true self, our true potential as well as our limitations. This gives us a much more realistic view of ourselves.

We are invited into a relationship through which we shall be transformed. This is not limited to a moral improvement but changes our whole perspective on reality and the way we relate to it. For our transformation to proceed, we must learn to accept the reality of ourselves and let go of the cherished illusions and defence mechanisms we have built up over the course of many years. Many people feel they are going backward when these kinds of thoughts begin to arise. They can think that silent prayer is not for them because as soon as they start to pray all they seem to experience is an unending flow of distractions. Actually this is a blessed time when we are being invited to let go of our own ideas, even of what prayer is, and allow the Spirit to pray within us. The number and nature of our thoughts have no effect whatever on the genuineness of our prayer. It may very well be that we are bombarded with thoughts when God is most actively at work within us cleansing out the caverns of our heart.

The prayer will be peaceful at times and at other times heavily laden with thoughts and emotions. Both experiences are part of the same process of integration and healing. Every kind of experience can therefore be accepted with the same peace, gratitude, and confidence in God. So if you are suffering from a barrage of thoughts, you do not have to articulate the sacred word clearly in your imagination or keep repeating it in a frantic effort to stabilize your mind. Think the sacred word as easily as you think any thought that comes to mind spontaneously. If you cannot do this, and the thoughts do not stop, do not worry. If your desire is to consent to the presence and action of God, how can it fail to be fruitful despite what you may feel?

The Four Rs

In the method of Centering Prayer all thoughts of whatever kind are dealt with in exactly the same way. Whenever you become aware of thoughts, return ever so gently to the sacred word as the symbol of your intention to consent to God's presence and action within. To help us remember how to deal with thoughts, we speak of the four Rs:

1. Resist no thought;
2. Retain no thought;
3. React emotionally to no thought;
4. Return ever so gently to the sacred word.

We do not try to keep back the flow of thoughts. That would be as futile as trying to halt the incoming tide. Thoughts are going to come no matter what we do, and we just have to get used to that fact. If we try to resist thoughts we are actually turning away from simply being in God's presence in order to fight the thoughts. Our intention just for that moment has shifted from consenting to the presence and action of God within to a desire to do battle with the particular thoughts that happen to be worrying us.

With particular thoughts it can be enticing to try to remember them for later. This again is shifting our intention, even if rather subtly. It can be difficult not to react emotionally to some types of emotionally-charged thoughts. For example, the thought of a recent argument may impose itself in our minds during the time of prayer. It would be very natural to become upset and carry on the argument in our head instead of simply consenting to be in God's presence. However, the advice is the same as with all kinds of thoughts—whenever you become aware that you are reacting simply return very gently to the sacred word. Do not get upset with yourself, as that is pointless. The fact that you react to emotionally-charged thoughts is not a sign that this kind of prayer is for more saintly people. It is simply an indication that you are human. The fact that you have thoughts does not matter, but what you do when you become aware that you are thinking instead of praying does. With all kinds of thoughts, whenever you become aware of them just return to the sacred word.

The intention to consent to God's presence and action is the heart and soul of the Centering Prayer method. Progress in Centering Prayer is most certainly not to arrive at a state when you have no thoughts but gradually to become detached from all thoughts. Detachment means not to stick to them, not to have them draw you away from where you want to be. The thoughts will still be present, but they will no longer have power over you. To be detached from all things is to be passionately concerned for them but to stand sufficiently apart from them so that they do not control you.

For all those people who have been troubled for years with distractions in prayer the good news is that there are no distractions in Centering Prayer unless you deliberately entertain thoughts, or if you get up and walk away. The key to dealing with thoughts in the method of Centering Prayer is to return ever so gently to the sacred word whenever you become aware of thinking instead of simply being in the presence of God.

Chapter Five

THE FRUIT OF CENTERING PRAYER

Why do we pray? What are we looking for from prayer?

Any relationship that moves beyond friendliness demands a commitment of some sort. There are many reasons why most of our relationships do not go very deep. We may not want to get deeply involved with some people, or we may not find our desires for depth in a relationship reciprocated. Because of the demands a friendship makes on us, we cannot cope with too many friends. We can cope with lots of acquaintances but not lots of friends in the proper sense of that term. One of the reasons why many of our relationships do not go very deep is that we tend to shy away from commitment. The inability to commit ourselves in human relationships will be reflected in our relationship with God.

The relationship with God requires a commitment that costs not less than everything. Faith must inform our values and affect how we live in this world and how we treat one another. When we realize and accept how much God loves us we will want to respond to this immense love.

It is like when a couple fall in love. It has been suggested that falling in love is nature's trick to entice people to make the commitment to each other required to provide the best atmosphere for nurturing children. Falling in love is a very powerful experience. The emotions explode, and we say and do things we would not normally do. The couple want to spend more and more time together. They may realize that they want to spend the rest of their lives together.

We can have a powerful experience of God's love that floods our senses and makes us desire God with a fervour we have never experienced before. We pray more and get much more out of prayer at this time. In our generosity we may set ourselves a prayer régime that is impossible to maintain. The feeling of loving God or of being in love with someone is not the same as actually loving them. Love involves commitment.

Few of us make a commitment with completely pure motives. We may think our motives are pure, but we are unconsciously pushed and pulled by hidden drives. Our unconscious motivations are very influential. A commitment is a process of growth and not something we do at any particular moment. At a marriage service the bride and groom make vows. They are vowing themselves to an ongoing process of growth. So we do not commit ourselves to another person only as he or she is at this present moment but to the person as he or she grows and develops over the years. Growth means change, and so as we live our commitment day by day we may have to adjust or change the ideas we had when we first made the commitment. This is part of the human condition, and the very fulfilling of the commitment strengthens us and enables us to mature. The difficulties of daily life will gradually reveal our true motives if we are prepared to accept the truth.

So do I love the other person or God for what I get out of the relationship, or do I simply love? The young couple who have fallen in love may agree to marry. In order to prepare a modern wedding, usually at least a year is required. During this time some couples will come to realize that they are not suited to each other and split up. This can cause heartache, but better the pain now rather than later. The time of preparation is crucial because the foundations for a real commitment are being put in place so that the relationship will last beyond the honeymoon.

In the relationship with God, not everything is revealed all at once. Neither does God expect perfection all at once.

Growing in friendship with the Lord, like any friendship, is a slow and gradual process. Our relationship with God will go through times of difficulty. Difficulties can be looked upon as purely negative events we must endure, or they can be understood as growth points. The love of the young couple must mature through living day by day with one another and coping together with the events of life. At times it might seem that the wonderful love of their wedding day has gone forever, but it has hopefully been replaced by a much deeper, richer, and more mature love.

The consent of the couple on their wedding day is a major commitment to each other, but obviously it is not the end of the story by any means. Their consent must be renewed day in and day out, especially in times of difficulty. A formal commitment to God was made at our baptism. Perhaps some of us remember that event, but for many of us the commitment was made by another on our behalf. At some stage we must really make that commitment our own. God will give himself totally only to those who give themselves totally to God. There are various levels of commitment, and sometimes we want to stay at one level when God is calling us to another more intimate level. Rarely will this refusal take place at a conscious level; if it does it will soon be repressed, because we do not want to think that we would refuse anything to God.

For any kind of commitment trust is required, but, as we know, trust does not come easily. This is why we need time to prepare for a commitment. In the case of the relationship with God we need time really to get to know God and to learn to trust. Often this will mean overcoming childish fears arising from ideas about God given to us as children. So we need to examine our ideas about God. How does the idea of total abandonment to God affect me? Do I really know deep within me that God loves me, or, if I am really honest with myself, am I just a little bit afraid of God? If that is the case I can examine the cause of my fear, bring it out into the daylight, and see it for what it is. We are called to believe the gospel, to accept the Good News Jesus brings, and to entrust ourselves to him. Remember that Jesus never condemned ordinary human frailties but only self-righteousness. Finally, we must let go of our fear and jump into the water. Ultimately it is fear that prevents us from making the total commitment required.

We do not normally examine ourselves too closely, and so we may very well be totally unaware of our fear of commitment. We can even deny that we are afraid and be convinced that we are right, but our behaviour will give us away if we stop for a moment to reflect on what we do and why we do it. We have various ways of seeking to escape from making a commitment. One way is to pretend that we have already made the commitment and that we do not have to do anything else. We can skim the surface of life and relationships without really getting in amongst it, without risking "getting our hands dirty." How do you react when someone challenges you to examine yourself really closely? Do you tend to change the subject quickly or do something to take your mind off the uneasy feeling arising within you? Do you become annoyed with the other person? Do you tend to get diverted easily from a difficult subject? Listen to yourself sometime.

Once you take on a really ascetical course of action, not just giving up sugar for Lent but actually tackling your hidden motivations head on by attempting to change the direction in which you are looking for happiness, you will discover that you more easily become uncomfortably aware of elements in your life that need looking at seriously. There will always be the tendency to run away from this battle, because it is very hard. However, we must trust that God really is on our side. God shows us little by little what is in us. God will never demand more from us than we are capable of giving, and our capacity is in itself a grace from God.

Humility is the foundation stone of the spiritual building. It involves knowing and accepting the truth about ourselves. We often think we are much better than we really are, and so being made aware of our reality can come as a profound shock to our system. We are asked to accept what is pointed out to us and to learn from it. It is a great help if we can look at ourselves with a bit of humour. We should not take ourselves too seriously. We are very funny creatures with our silly little pretensions. At the same time, pretentious though we may be, we are called to share in the intimate family life of God and to become like God.

We are also very subtle people, and so we can use very subtle ways to escape the commitment that costs not less than everything. We can be too busy to pray, for example: everything we have to do is vital, and prayer simply gets squeezed out by our everyday reality. I can convince myself that no one except me can do this or that or the other. Who is the saviour of the world? Will civilization as we know it collapse if I do not write this letter or attend that meeting or stop and dedicate twenty minutes of my precious time to God?

We started this chapter by asking, "Why do we pray?" and "What are we looking for from prayer?" The heart and the soul of Centering Prayer is the intention to consent to the presence and action of God. If you are looking for a relaxation exercise or a way of prayer that will make you feel good, do not take up the practice of Centering Prayer. Through this practice we are asking God to purify us of all selfishness, and therefore the greatest fruit of a regular practice of Centering Prayer is the purifying action of God in our lives. We may never become aware of what God is doing. In fact we may think we are wasting our time sitting being bombarded by the most mundane thoughts. Our initial ideas of what prayer is all about may very well undergo purification. The principal effects of Centering Prayer are experienced in daily life and not during the prayer itself.

One of the good things about Centering Prayer as a method is that it teaches us to let go of all thoughts. Anything, even very good and seemingly holy things, can distract us from the demands of the relationship with God. There is a great distinction between working for God and doing God's work. The former may seem excellent, but can in fact be a subtle way of avoiding the latter. Working for God means spending our energy doing what we think God wants, and we can be very generous in doing so. Doing God's work means doing what God actually wants—which may be the same but may also be very different. God's ways are not our ways, and God's thoughts are not our thoughts (Isa. 55:8). We may think we know what God wants or what God should want, but perhaps God's will is very different from our ideas. Jesus taught his disciples to pray that God's will be done, and before his passion he himself prayed earnestly, "Father, if you are willing, remove this cup from me, yet, not my will but yours be done" (Luke 22:42; Matt. 26:39; Mark 14:36). A fruit of a consistent practice of Centering Prayer may very well be a reforming of our will according to the will of God—not always pleasant but ultimately very rewarding. This of course is normally a very slow process—indeed lifelong.

If we are faithful to the practice of Centering Prayer as a way of consenting to God's presence and action in our lives we will become more and more attuned to God in daily life and more able to let go of the cherished notions about ourselves that have held us together for so many years. One reason for the strong stress on getting the recipe right is that even something like Centering Prayer can be used by the false part of us. I can decide for myself that I like this bit from Centering Prayer but that bit from something else and so make up my own method of prayer. There need be nothing wrong with this, but the danger is that I want to do my own thing, which is not a seeking of God but of oneself. Or perhaps I take up Centering Prayer so that I can teach it to my little prayer group. I will read a book, and that is enough because I am a quick learner! I don't need anyone else to tell me about how to pray! In this way Centering Prayer simply becomes just another string to my bow and not an encounter with the Living God.

The method of Centering Prayer is not intended to be rigid, but it does provide certain guidelines to help us stay in the silence with God. Silence can be difficult, and so we can try to escape because we are being called to let go at ever-deepening levels. We can while away twenty minutes or even an hour in a pleasant daydream or fast asleep. We can do our own thing during the time we set aside and call it Centering Prayer; but it is not, because we are not truly consenting to God's presence and action in our lives but rather doing what we want.

The spiritual journey is not a series of tasks to accomplish and then finish with. Remember the stages of *lectio*—read, reflect, respond, and rest. From time to time we shall have to return to something we thought we had dealt with, but now at a deeper level. So from time to time we may have to return to talking things over with God or reflecting or just letting our hearts speak to the heart of God. At the same time we need to persevere with the daily time for Centering Prayer, especially when things seem difficult, because that is often the sign that God is very active in our lives.

Commitment costs; there is no gain without pain. If I want something strongly enough I will do what is necessary to achieve it and not count the cost. We have all done difficult things in our lives without counting the cost because we have really desired to reach the goal we have set ourselves. In God is the fulfilment of every desire of our heart, and the gifts God will pour out are beyond anything we can ever imagine. "Give, and it will be given to you. A good measure, pressed down, shaken together, running over, will be put into your lap; for the measure you give will be the measure you get back" (Luke 6:38). God can never be outdone in generosity.

The practice of letting go of all thoughts at the time of prayer leads to the virtue of detachment, which means being in a right relationship with our environment. According to St John of the Cross and St Teresa of Avila, detachment is one of the most important of the virtues. We tend to define ourselves by our environment and so are afraid of letting go. Detachment means that we are gradually released from disordered attachments to people and things so that we can attain to the freedom of the children of God and others can be free also. The word "things" has a very broad sweep. It includes material things, ideas, feelings, emotions, and so forth. Material things are good and have been created for everyone's benefit, but we can so easily let things enslave our hearts. St John of the Cross said that it matters little whether a bird is tied down by a stout cord or a slender thread: it cannot fly in either case.[19] We too must attend to our own feelings and emotions. We ignore them at our peril, but if we allow ourselves to be driven by them we are not free. Suppressing emotions and feelings is very dangerous and ultimately fruitless, because they will keep emerging in one form or another until they are attended to. However, the faithful practice of Centering Prayer does help us to let go and be free with regard to our emotions. Gradually God can reveal to us our "hidden agenda"—what really motivates us, often without our being aware. When we have developed a habit of letting go we can begin to face ourselves as we are.

There is a tendency in us to try to possess people—to love them to death, as it were. We try to make people into things to gratify our own needs. We are called to love people as

God loves them, and this kind of love sets them free to be themselves whether that reality happens to please us or not. As we let go at various levels of our personality we can begin to stand in life-giving relationships to other people.

Detachment does not mean rejecting or despising things or people lest they in some way damage our precious relationship with God. That would be unchristian and inhuman. It does not mean denying that we have certain feelings and emotions or trying to repress them because we feel that they do not exactly fit the image we have built up of ourselves. Again, that is totally unhelpful to us. Feelings and emotions are neither good nor bad. Whatever they are, they must be accepted as part of us, perhaps a part we would rather not acknowledge, but nevertheless they are a very important part of us. Through the practice of Centering Prayer we are helped to accept ourselves just as we are, as God accepts us. God created us as human beings and not as angels. God's only Son became one of us, and therefore God knows by experience what it means to be human. We insult God if we try to repress our human nature, but we are called to walk to maturity, which means to become fully human and fully alive. Detachment is not indifference but a non-possessive attitude toward everything and everyone. This non-possessive attitude is symbolized at the time of prayer by returning ever so gently to the sacred word whenever we become aware of thoughts. This non-possessive attitude during prayer will flow into our daily lives.

There are certain stages of growth that we all must go through. Growth, we hope, does not end when we become physically adult but goes on at least until the moment of our death. Part and parcel of our human growth is what sometimes is called "the spiritual life." This is not something separate from the rest of life but affects and is affected by all other aspects of life. There are various stages of development in the Christian life. We may read about the great saints and wish we were like them, but we are not called to be like them. We are called to become saints in our own way; we are called to show forth the image of God in which we have been created. Each one of us has a special unique gift to reveal a particular facet of God through our own personality. We cannot become saints overnight. It is a long journey to arrive at the perfection of our own humanity. The Exodus is a good model for the journey each of us must undertake. The Israelites spent forty years in the desert before they were ready to enter the promised land, so we will not accomplish the journey overnight.

We cannot pass on from one stage of growth to another until we have dealt sufficiently with the issues that need to be dealt with at that point. However, there does come a moment when we do need to pass on and not linger. What is good at one point can actually become an obstacle at a later stage. We must abandon what is no longer helpful at the right time.

Letting go can be very painful, but we are asked to let go so that we can continue our journey unencumbered by many things. We are rather like a ship that needs to jettison its cargo in order to stay afloat and reach harbour. Growing up is painful, but it is very sad to refuse the invitation to grow and so remain childish.

We tend spontaneously to cling to people and to all sorts of things, thinking that they will bring us happiness. At some point in our lives we discover this is simply not true. It is a painful fact to face, but face it we must if we are to grow up. Centering Prayer helps us to sink into God and to rest there. In God we discover the source and goal of all our yearnings. In so doing we gradually come to realize the emptiness and uselessness of all our attachments. Nothing can ever satisfy us fully and completely save God alone. We find that our attachments are incompatible with our true purpose and present an obstacle to sinking into God. If we are seeking to open our very selves to God we shall discover that our attachments disturb us. We shall remain unhappy until we let them go. A good model for the truly free individual is St Francis of Assisi; he loved the whole of creation with great passion, but because of his great love for God he was not enslaved by things.

As we grow in our relationship with God we may discover that we can more easily let go of obvious attachments to things and to people, but then we have to deal with the rather more subtle attachments. Another fruit that can be expected from a faithful practice of Centering Prayer is a gradual growth in unconditional love. We tend to restrict our love in various ways, but the love of God is universal, and when we seek to rest in God we learn how to love from the source of all love. As we let go of our narrow vision of who deserves to be loved we gradually learn to look on people as God looks on them. We learn compassion and respect for the freedom of others. People can then begin to be set free by our love and not entangled in an emotional web. We no longer only find God in people; we begin to find people in God. God holds each person very close, and when we rest in the heart of God we learn to love as God does.

How we actually treat other human beings regardless of class, race, religion, sex, age, or education becomes the test of how religious we are and how deep our friendship with God is. Our religious maturity is not measured by ecstasies, trances, visions, vigils, or feelings of peace but by how consistently we treat others with fairness and equality. We are followers of Jesus in as much as we love others as he has loved us.

The transformation process in us is intensified by our being faithful to the daily encounter with God. God desires to make saints of us, but we often hamper God's work by refusing to let go of some of our own ideas. No one can teach us to swim if we refuse to let go of rail. If we do let go of the rail we still cannot swim, but we are now more likely to be able to learn. We must still let go of various other fears before we can learn. We must let go of the fear of drowning and trust ourselves to the instructor. Centering Prayer teaches us to let go of the fear of the unknown and to trust ourselves radically to God, who alone can save us. This radical trust makes the process much quicker. If we had total trust in the swimming instructor, knowing that he or she would never let us drown, we would learn to swim in a very short space of time. Just so, Centering Prayer teaches us to trust. God then can heal the roots of sin more quickly and bring the new self to birth.

What we are doing in Centering Prayer is aiming at God, who alone can fulfil every desire of our hearts. We cannot make our lives fruitful: this is the work of God, who desires to transform us. Once we are transformed we shall bear abundant fruit that will last. The fruit of the Spirit's action in our lives is "love, joy, peace, patience, kindness, generosity, faithfulness, gentleness and self control" (Gal. 5:22-3). No amount of gritting our teeth and trying to produce this fruit ourselves will bring it about. It is the work of God's Holy Spirit. If we let go and entrust our lives to God we shall be melted, moulded, filled, and used for the benefit of many, and in this we shall find our joy.

We are being called to surrender to God, whose name is Love. As the Prophet says:

> When love beckons you, follow him,
> Though his ways are hard and steep.
> And when his wings enfold you yield to him,
> Though the sword hidden in his pinions may wound you.
> And when he speaks to you believe in him,
> Though his voice may shatter your dreams
> As the north wind lays waste the garden.
> For even as love crowns you so shall he crucify you.
> Even as he is for your growth so is he for your pruning.

> Even as he ascends to your heights and caresses
> Your tenderest branches that quiver in the sun,
> So shall he descend to your roots and shake them
> In their clinging to the earth.[20]

If we do our best to remain faithful to God in daily life and in prayer we shall become increasingly open and receptive to the divine inspiration. There is no limit to this process because God is infinite, and we are invited to continue the journey to its fullest expression. This is a journey into God's world, in which God can do anything; it is not the limited world of our own work, plans, and capabilities. It is a journey of sheer faith, and so its progress is imperceptible to our normal ways of knowing.

If we are going to learn a language we must work at it. There is no other way. Because the language of silence is difficult to learn, we are sometimes tempted to turn off the road for a while. If we turn off the road to chase after thoughts we may find it difficult to get back on. So resist no thought, retain no thought, and react to no thought. In Centering Prayer return ever so gently to the sacred word.

Pray as you can; do not attempt to pray as you cannot. If you feel called to move beyond your own thoughts and meditations and simply rest in God, follow that inspiration. When you go to a foreign country you may understand nothing at first; that can be quite frustrating, but gradually you will begin to recognize some words and then phrases. You have to stay with it and not give up. If you feel called to enter into silence stay with it—or rather stay with God, who is revealed in the silence. When you begin to hear the silent music no other music will satisfy you.

We need relationships. The experience of intimacy with another expands and deepens our capacity to relate to God and to everyone else. Receiving is a very delicate way of loving. This method of prayer puts other kinds of prayer into a fresh perspective: prayer then becomes more of a personal relationship.

Chapter Six

CENTERING PRAYER AND CONTEMPLATIVE PRAYER

All prayer is a response to God, who takes the initiative. Centering Prayer is a method of prayer designed to open us to the gift of contemplative prayer. Centering Prayer is a way of simplifying our activity at the time of prayer, a way of moving beyond the spontaneous outpouring of our hearts to the experience of "resting" in God. It is a way of waiting upon God with love, not paying particular attention to words, concepts, images, or symbols but just maintaining the intention to be in God's presence and to consent to God's purifying action in our lives.

Love is an intention of the will and not primarily a feeling, and so the emotions are not a good indicator of how the relationship with God is developing. At a certain stage on our journey lack of emotions at the time of prayer can actually be a sign of great growth. In the method of Centering Prayer we do not latch on to any emotion or feeling but simply seek to be in God's presence. Our activity in the period of Centering Prayer is very delicate, returning, whenever we become aware that we are thinking, to the sacred word as the symbol of our intention to say "yes" to God.

Some people have difficulty with Centering Prayer because they do not seem to be doing anything, not realizing that consenting is in itself a great work. Prayer is much more than what we do, say, or think. Prayer is the work of the Holy Spirit in us and the door through which we actually encounter God. At the beginning, just as in a human relationship, we tend to use many words and be very active in prayer, but as we mature in our relationship with God our words, thoughts, and activity are gradually put to sleep as we learn to relate to God on another level. God is far greater than our most brilliant thoughts. At the beginning of a relationship with God it is right and necessary to reflect, but it is also important to realize that our reflections cannot confine God. At some point we shall be drawn to silence, to stillness, so that God can speak to our hearts. God's voice is very gentle. The story of the manifestation of God to the Prophet Elijah is very instructive.[21] Elijah escapes the clutches of those who are seeking his life, goes into the desert, and wishes he were dead, but God will not allow him to give up. God sends an angel to strengthen him with food for the journey to Mount Horeb, the holy mountain. It is there that God comes to Elijah not in the earthquake or the great fire or the mighty wind, which were the expected accompaniments of God in the Hebrew scriptures. Instead Elijah met God in the sound of a gentle breeze. God came to him in a completely unexpected way and in silence.

Jesus Christ is the word of God. God spoke this word in the silence of eternity, and it is only in silence that we can truly hear this word. The chosen people were prepared to receive the Messiah, but when he did come he was largely rejected. The people clearly could not understand what God was saying to them; they could not understand God's language. Like any language, God's language is difficult to understand if we do not know it. Learning another language is not at all easy, but the effort involved does pay great dividends. God's normal language is silence. Some silence can be empty, but the silence of God is filled with meaning.

Only God can teach us the language of silence. In a way it is rather like learning to appreciate classical music. We can learn the characteristic sounds of different instruments and study musical theory, but either something happens inside or it does not. Some people hate classical music, some find it boring, some quite like some of it, and some find a whole world of meaning in it. Other people can help us to appreciate classical music but cannot make us do so. They cannot make us love it as they do. We shall of course never come to appreciate classical music if we never listen to it: nothing can take the place of the personal experience. So we must experience the silent music in which God speaks to the human heart in ways that transcend the power of human speech to describe. This cannot be taught; it can only be experienced. Centering Prayer is a method of prayer designed to reduce the barriers, especially those within us, to hearing this silent music.

Centering Prayer is also a way of putting ourselves in the way of the divine action. All of us have obstacles to God within us, which lumped together can be called "the false self." This false self is unique to each of us, and so the action of God will vary in each individual. The Spirit, like the slow drip of water on rock, gradually begins to wear these obstacles down. Sometimes this drip can seem like a torrent! Centering Prayer is nothing other than consenting to the presence and action of God. It is a way of saying, "yes, yes, yes" to this movement of the Spirit.

In the method of Centering Prayer we are just there waiting for God. Gradually this habit of "waiting" begins to predominate. We may think we are in no man's land. There may sometimes be a sense of knowing, but most of the time we do not know. We wonder whether we have been asleep. Have we been praying correctly? Will these thoughts never end?

By consenting to allow oneself to be in this no man's land or nowhere place, the Spirit and our spirit meet every now and again, and this is the beginning of contemplative prayer. Some writers use the concept "acquired contemplation" to mean a level of silence the human spirit can reach—aided, of course, by the grace of God. Often the terms "contemplation" and "contemplative prayer" are also used for this state. However, here these terms are reserved for the time when our activity, no matter how simple, comes to an end and God takes over. When this happens, how this happens, is shrouded in mystery. We cannot pinpoint a moment when our prayer becomes contemplation. All we do is consent to God's presence and action within and leave the rest to God.

Once we begin to talk of contemplative prayer, every word is basically a metaphor. We are talking around an indescribable event. Contemplation is a kind of being-to-being conversation with no intermediary. In contemplation God does not come through the senses or through the normal pattern of knowing. God comes by an unknown way, creeps up on us, as it were, and often takes us by surprise. It is a knowledge of God that is impregnated with love, and this knowledge is infused directly into our being, our centre, in such a way that the individual does not know how it got there. The basic human way of learning anything is through our senses, and we are taught to conceptualize and rationalize. This is very good training and necessary in order to get on with life. Theological and biblical studies are also very useful, but if they remain head knowledge they will not be of great benefit to us. If, on the other hand, the study of the things of God motivates us to enter a personal relationship with God it will bear abundant fruit. However, we usually bring our basic approach to life into our prayer and so cannot "see" the mystery because we are looking in the wrong direction. In contemplation our normal ways of knowing and understanding are stilled, and at first there can be a feeling of anxiety that we are doing nothing. So contemplation is a strange new land where everything natural to us seems to be turned upside down, where we learn the language of silence.

It is a new way of being—not doing but simply being where our thoughts and concepts, our imagination, senses, and feelings are abandoned for faith in what is unseen and unfelt, where God's seeming absence to our senses is God's presence, and God's silence to our ordinary perception is God's speech. It is entering into the unknown, letting go of everything familiar we cling to for security. Entering this new land is at first like entering into darkness and emptiness. Yet a new life is growing in that darkness and emptiness. It is entering into a process that is a kind of death—death to our false self—and a rising to new life, to a new consciousness.

Contemplation is given: we are the receivers. Our job is to keep the receiver tuned in, not to try to grasp hold of whatever God wants to communicate to us. If we try to grasp hold of it, it will elude us. As St John of the Cross says: "So delicate is this refreshment that ordinarily if one desires or cares to experience it, one does not do so; for, as I say, it does its work when the soul is most at ease and free from care; it is like the air which, if one would close one's hand upon it, escapes."[22]

The discipline of the practice of Centering Prayer is meant as an aid to help us be present to the here and now with God. It is not contemplative prayer but a way to prepare ourselves to receive this gift if and when God desires to grant it. In Centering Prayer the curtain, so to speak, is brought down on our normal ways of knowing and feeling our way to God. It is a prayer of faith in which we let go of our memories, imagination, cognitive senses, emotional judgments, feelings of hope, despair, fear, anger, desire, aversion, love, hate, joy, or sorrow. These are not resisted or rejected but disregarded during the time of prayer so that we can open to the mystery within.

All prayer is our way of responding to God's invitation to an intimate relationship of friendship. To pray solely in order to get something, even something spiritual, is to seek the consolations of God instead of the God of consolations. Certainly in the method of Centering Prayer there is no particular goal in mind, such as having no thoughts or experiencing peaceful feelings or achieving some sort of spiritual experience. The heart and the soul of Centering Prayer is the intention to consent to God's presence and action. We believe that it is God's will to bring us into the intimate life of the Trinity, and this involves us in being transformed. It is vital that we consent to this process, and the work of transformation is greatly assisted by contemplative prayer. Centering Prayer is simply one way to open ourselves to the gift of contemplation. We need not worry if or when our prayer becomes contemplative; that is God's business. All we can do is co-operate with the will of God in every way we know and consent to the purifying action of God in our prayer and our daily life.

Chapter Seven

EXTENDING INTO DAILY LIFE

Any method of prayer is useful only insofar as it helps us grow in our relationship with God. If this relationship with God is growing it will affect every aspect of life. Centering Prayer is not simply a method of prayer one uses once or twice a day; it is a spiritual discipline of which the method is only one part. First, Centering Prayer is not at all intended to replace other kinds of prayer. We must continue to relate to God in whatever way we can, using all the means available. It is likely that a faithful practice of Centering Prayer will give new meaning to our traditional devotions. Since the teaching on Centering Prayer comes out of the lectio divina tradition, it fits naturally with a regular reading of the Bible and indeed helps us to enter deeper into the scriptures or gives us another view of them. The scriptures are not only stories about people of long ago; they are God's word to each of us here and now. Even when we have very little time we can glance at the Gospels and take a word or a phrase to think about as we continue with our daily tasks. The more we listen to God in the silence of our hearts, the more aware we shall be of God speaking to us in the scriptures. If the silence is not to be empty, we must not neglect the nourishment God provides for us throughout the day.

It is essential to be faithful to a daily encounter with God. Many people say that they simply have no time for prayer. This may indeed be true, but such a statement simply informs others of their priorities. We make time for what we really want to do. It may be that we do not have lots of leisure time to pray, but a great deal of time is not required. As a guideline, in the Centering Prayer practice, people are asked to pray for two twenty-minute periods each day. This is simply a guideline, so when it is not possible one must do what one can. Prayer is our response to God's call. God does not need the time; we do. God can do wonders without us but normally seeks our co-operation. By giving time to God we show that we are serious about the spiritual journey. We need to be on the lookout for opportunities to spend time with God, and we need to be creative in using those opportunities. However, what really matters is our intention. If we desire with all our heart that God take possession of us, seek to live this out in practice, and are willing to accept the consequences, then all shall be well. God is never outdone in generosity.

Spiritual formation is also important. Many people today seem to prefer a "pic'n'mix" religion, taking a bit from here and another bit from there. The spiritual formation of very many Christians seems to be limited to what they learned in school and from the Sunday sermon. The Centering Prayer practice emerges from and is enriched by the Christian contemplative tradition, and practitioners are encouraged to immerse themselves in the tradition whenever possible. The Christian contemplative tradition contains the wisdom of centuries and the experience of the great saints. It is available for all those who have ears to hear and who are willing to make an effort to learn more about their faith. While great intelligence and education are most certainly not requirements for a deep relationship with God, neither is culpable ignorance. Everyone is entitled to his or her opinion, but opinions based on thin air would be derided in any other area of life. There are many ways available to deepen one's knowledge of the Christian faith. One of these ways is through Contemplative Outreach, which focuses on the Christian contemplative tradition, teaching *lectio divina*, the most traditional way to foster an intimate relationship with

God, and Centering Prayer, which is a modern method of prayer with roots deeply embedded in the tradition.

Thomas Keating has succeeded in taking the best insights from this tradition and bringing them into dialogue with the insights of modern psychology. Psychology is a relatively modern science, and its discoveries about the human psyche have helped modern men and women to understand themselves better. Christians cannot turn the clock back and pretend that psychology does not exist or that it has no bearing on spirituality. While not every psychological theory is consonant with the Christian vision, many are, and it would be foolish indeed not to use some of their insights to assist us in our relationship with God. We can be like the wise scribe, praised by Jesus, who brings out of his treasure what is old and what is new (Matt. 13:52).

Psychology cannot provide all the answers to life's questions, but it can help us discover a lot more about ourselves. Growing closer to God is not just a matter of doing holy things but of consenting to God's presence and action in our lives. The purpose of the spiritual journey is that we may be transformed by God. God gradually reveals us to ourselves, and humility means to know and accept the truth about ourselves. Psychology can help us see far more about ourselves than just what appears on the surface.

The contemplative tradition is not easily accessible to everyone, and when some of the texts are actually read they can be very difficult to understand, or they can be misunderstood because of the vast cultural gap between the authors and our present day. The authors of the classic texts of Christian spirituality were dealing with the fundamental issues of the divine-human relationship that touch every generation of Christians. They naturally expressed themselves in terms of their own culture and education. We can only read them in terms of our culture, which includes the influence of psychology.

It is one thing to know the tradition and another to allow that knowledge to affect one's daily life. In the early Christian centuries many went into the desert in order to deepen their relationship with God and to do battle with what hindered this relationship. Of course it is not necessary to go into the desert to find God, because God lives within each of us. God upholds us at every moment, and every breath we take is a gift of God, who is closer to us than we can imagine. If we love someone it is natural to think of that person from time to time throughout the day. A very important way of extending the effects of one's prayer into daily life is to bring to mind that we are in the presence of God. It is not only spiritual things that can be shared with God. If God truly desires to have an intimate friendship with me, surely that means I should feel free to share with God what is important to me and indeed all the ups and downs of daily life. St Teresa of Avila said that God walks among the pots and pans, which means that God is to be found in the ordinary things of life. We can talk to God about whatever concerns us and so we become more aware of God's presence in our daily lives.

It is not easy to practise the presence of God because our minds and hearts are so filled with other things. The pressures of modern life make it understandable to forget all about God for lengthy periods of time. Some people find they need helps to remind them that wherever they happen to be they are in the presence of God.

One way that may help is to keep a little notebook nearby in which we can jot down some thought that has inspired us, perhaps from the scriptures or from a favourite book. It can be very useful to glance at these now and again, especially at those times when we think we must be mad to take the spiritual journey so seriously! The thoughts that inspired us in the past can serve to remind us why we originally set out on the spiritual journey and give us courage to continue.

Another way many generations have found helpful is that of active prayer. This comes from the Christian contemplative tradition above all through the teaching of John Cassian, a fourth-century monk who had an enormous influence on the development of monastic spirituality in the West. He was aware that he was simply passing on the wisdom of the desert which he himself had gleaned from his discussions with many holy men and women. He quotes one such holy man, Abba Isaac, who gave a prayer formula to help banish unwanted thoughts and keep the mind fixed on God. The formula he proposed was taken from Psalm 69 (70): "Oh God, come to my aid. Lord make haste to help me."[23] This formula is used at the beginning of the Divine Office. Such a formula, or other words, especially from the scriptures, has been found very helpful in extending the fruit of one's prayer time into the hurly-burly of daily life. We can perhaps use a favourite phrase from the Bible to remind us throughout our day that we are always in the presence of God.

Another great tradition stemming from the same source is that of the Jesus Prayer, which was made popular in the West through the book *The Way of the Pilgrim*. Because of the great difficulty of controlling thoughts at the time of prayer, the Eastern ascetic tradition proposed taking refuge in the name of Jesus by the continual and rhythmic repetition of a short prayer calling on the Lord's help.

If we choose an active prayer, we can say it from time to time throughout the day and thus allow it to sink into us so that it arises naturally within us, especially in times of stress. Therefore the active prayer is the phrase that reminds us of the presence of God. You will find a list of suggested traditional active prayers in Appendix 2, but any phrase that reminds us that God is truly with us will serve. The active prayer is also useful to cut across the commentaries that arise within us whenever we become upset. On these occasions all our good intentions often fly out the window. Sometimes we are advised to "count to ten." The active prayer can have a similar effect of giving us time to cool down, but it has the very important additional element of reminding us that we are in the presence of God. Being aware of this may make us less likely to vent our anger on someone else.

The thought that each human being has been created in the image and likeness of God is closely related to the idea that we are constantly in God's presence. Each human being reveals some aspect of God to those who have eyes to see. Admittedly, perceiving the presence of God in some, if not all, people is very difficult, but the very effort to do so will pay dividends. Of course we shall fail often, but failure need not prevent us from further effort.

The whole of creation speaks of its Creator. It is not so difficult to be aware of God's majesty on a beautiful day, but a grey and wet winter's night is another matter. However, even being caught in a downpour can remind us of God's abundant generosity in sending the rain on the good and bad alike— though in this instance we may have preferred God to be generous elsewhere and not on top of us! There are many things in life about which we can do nothing. Many of our difficulties stem not so much from what happens to us but from our reaction to these events. If I miss the bus, being upset is not going to help the situation, but if I allow it to, this relatively minor event can ruin my entire day. A positive acceptance of what I cannot change is a good way of maintaining one's equilibrium throughout the day. The "Serenity Prayer" comes to mind:

> "Lord grant me the serenity to accept the things I cannot change,
> the courage to do something about the things I can change and the wisdom to know the difference."

This attitude can come into play in situations more serious than missing the bus or getting soaked. Acceptance is not a passive or submissive attitude to life. Every day many things happen that should not be passively accepted. We should not accept the existence of grinding poverty or injustice. While Jesus invited his followers to turn the other cheek, we are not expected to be doormats. We need to ask God to give us the courage to do something about the things we can and should change. As the prayer says, we need also the wisdom to know the difference between what we can and what we cannot change.

Prayer is valuable in itself, since it is the way we relate to God. Petitionary prayer is important in that by expressing our needs to God we remind ourselves that we are creatures and that we depend on God for everything. The Lord's Prayer itself is a model for petitionary prayer: our first concern must be for the coming of God's Kingdom and that God's will be done. Prayer is valuable not only for its effects, but these too are important. The most important effect is that our will is gradually conformed to God's. Through our prayer we take on the mind and heart of Christ.

It is vital that our prayer really be an opening to the love of God. The desire of our heart is the crucial factor. "Not everyone who says to me, 'Lord, Lord' will enter the kingdom of heaven but only the one who does the will of my Father in heaven" (Matt. 7:21). Because of the human condition our desires are rarely pure. Many less worthy elements enter in, but that is not an insurmountable problem. God will heal us if we desire, but we must first recognize that we need healing. More than once, before Jesus carries out a healing he asks those involved whether they want to be healed. In the story of the healing of the blind man (Mark 10:46-52), Jesus is approached by the man, who asks for mercy. Jesus looks at the man and asks him what he would have Jesus do for him. This seems a rather strange question because the answer is surely obvious, but this story is part of the early teaching on baptism, signifying that the physical blindness of the man represents a more serious ailment—spiritual blindness. Before being healed, the man must recognize his blindness and his true desire: "Lord, that I may see!"

The effect of prayer is not to make us feel good or holy but to transform us. Christ is the prototype of the new humanity, and the process of transformation is to conform us to Christ. This is the perfection of our humanity. However, this is a long process and perhaps only reaches its goal in the kingdom of heaven. Jesus did not wait until his disciples were perfect to send them out to preach the good news. He called all sorts of people—fishermen, zealots, tax collectors. He sent them out with very little: "Take no gold or silver or copper in your belts, no bag for your journey, or two tunics, or sandals, or a staff . . ." (Matt. 10:9-10). These disciples made many mistakes, and occasionally Jesus was exasperated with them. James and John wanted to call down fire from heaven on a town when they did not find the acceptance which they thought was their due (Luke 9:54). They also wanted special privileges in the kingdom of heaven; they argued among themselves about who was the greatest; and finally they all ran away just when Jesus needed them most. Despite all these human frailties, Jesus entrusted them with an important mission. So with us, God does not wait until we are transformed before giving us a mission but entrusts us with it before we are ready. Like the disciples who set out with just the clothes on their back, we need to set out trusting in God.

The quality of our prayer, of our relationship with God, will determine the quality of our Christian service. Every Christian is called to mission. The particular service to which each of us is called depends on our possibilities but above all on the choice of God, who "chooses the weak and makes them strong in bearing witness to Him."[24] The relationship with God is an intimate, personal relationship, but like any healthy relationship it does not exclude others but makes the person more able to relate. A growing relationship with God will make us more aware of the needs of others.

The acid test of the health of our relationship with God is how we treat our neighbour. "How does God's love abide in anyone who has the world's goods and sees a brother or sister in need and yet refuses help? Little children, let us love, not in word or speech but in truth and action" (1 John 3:17-18). The way of prayer leads us to see reality as if with the eyes of God and to love the whole of creation as if with the heart of God.

When we become aware of the demands of the Christian vocation, we may very well feel like running away. At this juncture we need to remember the promise of Jesus: "Come to me, all you that are weary and are carrying heavy burdens, and I will give you rest. Take my yoke upon you, and learn from me; for I am gentle and humble in heart, and you will find rest for your souls. For my yoke is easy, and my burden is light" (Matt. 11:28-30). The yoke of Christ is easy because God does not demand great things from us but only our consent. St Teresa of Avila said that God does not look so much at the magnitude of anything we do as at the love with which we do it.[25]

We cannot change the world or even one other person, but we can change ourselves. Thomas Keating tells the story of the young man who lived a dissolute life and whose greatest pleasure was to spend every evening in the pub, where he would prove his manhood by regularly drinking his friends under the table. Possibly thanks to his mother's prayers, this young man underwent a dramatic conversion. He went back to church, which he had not entered for a long time, and he felt a great attraction to spiritual things. He wanted to give his whole life to God and finally decided to enter the Trappists, one of the most austere religious Orders in the Catholic Church. Lent arrived, and the great monastic fast began. All the monks began with fervour, but one by one, beginning with the older ones, they began to drop out and were given permission to eat a little extra for the sake of their health. At the end of Lent only one monk had kept the rigorous fast. You've guessed it—our friend! On Easter Day the same feelings of pride surged up from the bottom of his heart as he used to experience in the pub. Instead of drinking his friends under the table, he was now fasting them under the table! This young man had changed a great deal about himself—where he lived, what he worked at, what he wore, his hairstyle, and even his moral behaviour—but his heart remained the same. In a religious exterior there still beat a worldly heart.

One of the important contributions Thomas Keating has made to modern spirituality is to explain an age-old problem in terms modern people can understand, and he gives them the possibility of actually doing something about it. The problem can be put in different ways: How do we extend our experience of prayer into daily life? Or why does our prayer not seem to have much effect on our daily life? Why is it that we can pray and attend church for years without this having any discernible effect on our lives?

The following chapter sets out to examine this phenomenon, which touches on the fundamental problem of the human condition—what Thomas Keating and others have called "the false self."

Chapter Eight

THE FALSE SELF

At the start of his ministry, Jesus asked people to repent and believe the gospel (Mark 1:14-15). Being sorry for our sins is a part of repentance but is far from the whole story. The word used in the Gospel means literally "turn around in the road," so in order really to respond to what Jesus is asking of us we must stop and take a good look at our lives. We need to be as realistic as possible. If we think that, apart from one or two fairly minor faults, basically we are doing all right, then we are not going to understand the need for radical change in our lives. We are not going to understand the need to change direction.

The fundamental fact of our existence is that God lives within us. In John's Gospel, Jesus says that he is the vine and we are the branches and that if we live in him and he in us we will produce abundant fruit, for apart from him we can do nothing (John 15:5). St Teresa's image of the human soul as a castle with many mansions has become a classic of Christian spirituality. In the centre of this castle, in the most interior room, dwells God Alone. However, as Teresa goes on to say, many people live completely unaware that at the centre of their being lives God. This centre is our true self, which is often hidden by many layers of falsity. Jesus' invitation to repentance involves us in first becoming aware that we are not what we could be.

Jesus did not try to pull the wool over the eyes of his disciples. He made it very clear what could or would be involved in following him. He told them, "If any want to become my followers, let them deny themselves and take up their cross and follow me. For those who want to save their life will lose it and those who lose their life for my sake will find it."[26] This is the price of discipleship. Many have paid that price literally. Some people believe that we are on the verge of a new springtime for Christianity because the signs of the times point to the fact that God is purifying the Church and bringing it back to the purity of its origins. One of these signs is the return of the age of martyrdom, which was a mark of the primitive Church. Many people in our own day have paid with their lives for their faith in Jesus Christ. However, for most of us that fate does not seem likely at present. Far more likely is that we will be smothered by apathy. If then literal martyrdom seems unlikely, what can Christ be saying to us? What can it mean to deny ourselves, take up our cross and lose our life?

The greatest commandment for Christians is of course the double-sided commandment to love God with our whole heart, mind, and strength and to love our neighbour as ourselves.[27] Love involves sacrifice and self-denial, but this is easier spoken about than put into practice. There is a flaw in human beings, often referred to as original sin, which inclines us to selfishness. Sometimes even our best actions are marred by selfish motives, though these can often be hidden from us. The whole thrust of the writings of St John of the Cross describes the spiritual journey that begins when the individual responds to God's call to move away from self-love toward a truly disinterested love, which means a love that seeks the best for the other and does not cling or manipulate. We begin the spiritual journey distorted and in need of healing. The spiritual journey is about welcoming the love of God into our lives, love that transforms us and empties us of our limited and imperfect human ways of thinking, loving, and acting, changing them into divine ways.

What is wrong with our human ways of thinking, loving, and acting? They are limited and imperfect because we are human. They are subject to distortion by our selfish tendencies and as a result they are manifestations of the false self. It is this self that we need to deny, which must die so that we can find our true selves. To begin to face the false self and its destructive effects within us is to take to heart Jesus' message to repent and believe in the good news. Repentance could be said to mean to change the direction in which we are looking for happiness, to move away from self-love and direct ourselves toward God in whom alone lasting happiness is to be found. The false self emerges from what could be called the human condition. We are born into an imperfect world. Even if we are so fortunate as to have the best family there ever was, it is still not perfect since it is made up of fallible human beings. We are born very fragile with certain instinctual needs that are God-given and therefore good in themselves. These needs can be summed up under three headings:

1. The need for love and affection;
2. The need to survive;
3. The need for control.[28]

The need for affection affects how we think others perceive us, makes us desire to belong, to feel valued, needed, and loved. The basic instinct to survive affects how we perceive the trustworthiness of reality. Do we feel secure or are we in a threatening environment? The need to have some control over our own lives affects how we treat others. Do we try to control other people's lives? The instinctual needs are God-given, natural, good, and indeed essential, but when they are not satisfied they become demands. Happiness is equated with the prompt and constant fulfillment of these demands, and around them is grouped a complex of emotions that work together to get us what we want. These are rather like computer programmes. One action can set off a whole series of responses, and our emotional responses are designed to bring us happiness through the satisfaction of our demands.

Eventually these emotional programmes for happiness become exaggerated into centres of motivation that often work in us while we are unaware of their effect on our behaviour. In this way even what we think completely selfless actions can be driven by unconscious selfish motives.

Our false self is formed by compensatory behaviour, through which we seek to protect ourselves from real or imagined deprivations in regard to our needs for affection, survival, or control. The false self seeks happiness in over-compensating these needs. If we feel our instinctual needs are not being fulfilled we try to make sure they will be through our behaviour. This then becomes a pattern of behaviour so ingrained in us that we fail to see it, even though it is damaging us and other people and undoubtedly seriously limits our freedom to choose gospel values. This is the human condition in which we all share. Because of the fragility of childhood, the instinctual needs are not always fulfilled. Frustrations are sometimes unintentional or simply unavoidable or result from neglect or indifference of the parent.

The false self is an amalgamation of all the energies that gather around the basic needs for affection, survival, and control to satisfy them. On a level we are usually unaware of, we believe we shall be happy if these needs are met. The trouble is that everyone wants the same things, and the law of averages means that we cannot all get what we want. If we feel that we have been deprived of anything we believe we need to make us happy, we shall be upset in some way. Until we address the issue of the false self we shall be pushed around by our emotions, which reveal to us what is really going on inside us despite what we may like to think.

Let us now examine more closely these three fundamental needs to see how they can affect us in daily life and go toward the formation of the false self. The authors make no pretence to be psychologists but present what follows on the basis of common sense and what seems to be helpful for a deeper understanding of the human condition.

1. Need for love and affection

Human beings need to be loved. No matter how wonderful parents are, however, they are still human and therefore limited. Babies demand instant satisfaction of their needs and, when this satisfaction is not forthcoming quickly enough and constantly enough, perceive that the love is limited or conditional. This of course is not a rational but an emotional response. Babies cannot reason that the lack of instant gratification may very well be quite understandable. All they know is that they are not receiving the cuddles and caresses that are signs of being loved. Human beings need to be loved unconditionally, but only God can give us the love we crave. To be loved in a human way is wonderful but limited and conditioned simply because it is human. We are limited and fallible creatures and cannot respond perfectly at all times. That is the human condition. Also, the world in which we live presents us with situations over which we have little or no control. Children may feel deprived of love through no fault whatsoever of their parents. All of us carry wounds because of the fragility of childhood.

We pick up the very subtle and often unconscious messages from our environment that tell us what we must do and what we must avoid in order to be loved. We internalize these messages, and they become a part of us. They mould how we relate to other people so that they will approve of us, so that we will feel loved and accepted. We learn that if we are "good," people will approve of us, like us, and love us. We may then learn a pattern of behaviour whereby we become "people-pleasers," doing what we believe others will approve of rather than what is right. Those who are caught up in this behaviour can find its fault very difficult to spot. It can very well appear to be very Christian behaviour, since the individual concerned is always most helpful and eager to please others. The problem lies not with the behaviour in itself but with the motives behind it. It is one thing to be urged by the love of Christ to help someone in need and another to give gifts or lavish praise because of one's own need for acceptance. It is possible for these actions to appear similar at a superficial glance, but in fact, driven by our own needs, they use the other person as a thing to satisfy us. A more penetrating look at the behaviour of or simply being with the person concerned for some time will generally reveal whether the true motive is pure love or not. We may also learn that, whatever we do, we cannot gain the approval and love of others. In this case we will tend to be hostile toward others, rejecting their attempts to reach out to us. If we have been hurt by what our emotions perceived to be rejection in the past we may tend to be "prickly," not allowing others near us. In adulthood, when our emotions perceive any situation that shows similarities to those of childhood, the feeling of rejection will be triggered, with its accompanying feelings of fear and hostility, causing us to act in accordance with our learned behaviour.

2. Need for survival

We are born with an instinct for survival, which is healthy and good. We need a certain amount of security in our lives, and by this instinct we seek to protect ourselves from perceived danger and to make sure that what makes life possible and bearable is readily available. If, as children, we perceive a lack of security in our lives, we will seek as much security as possible because we do not like the feeling of unease that arises within us when some symbol of security is missing. A symbol of security is that which represents security to us. This can be valuable in itself or completely worthless. The important thing is what we feel about it. We can then pile up security symbols to make us feel better. Many children have a security blanket. As we get older we can let go of the physical blanket but replace it with something else we use to give us security in a very threatening world. Religion is a classic security blanket.

If for any reason, real or imagined, we felt deprived of security as a young child we may try to overcompensate for this in later life by acquiring as many as we can of the security symbols our culture provides. For some people these may be lots of money and those things money can buy. In a work environment a security symbol may be a bigger office or the latest gadget. In a religious culture the security symbols may be things we believe will protect us from evil and misfortune. None of these symbols is of course wrong in itself. The problem lies in the emotions we invest in these symbols. No amount of security symbols will completely satisfy our need for security, and whenever our demands are frustrated or our symbols are in some way threatened our emotional response will be an upsetting emotion—anger, grief, or jealousy.

3. Need for control

Slavery is universally condemned, at least in theory. Civilized legal systems recognize that human beings have certain rights to control their own lives. As babies we need the care and protection of parents and guardians, but before we are very old we begin to assert our individuality and exercise control in limited ways. As we grow up we take more and more control of our lives. Clearly this is a good instinct and necessary if we are to become responsible members of society. However, a problem may arise if we have felt deprived of control at an early age. This feeling can emerge from a real or imagined deprivation. The tendency then is to over-compensate and to develop a need always to be in control, becoming manipulative and domineering and needing to be right in every situation. If we feel uneasy or angry when we believe things are out of control or when others are questioning our opinion, these emotions may point to a distortion in our need for some control and power in our lives.

Sources of motivation form around our instinctual needs.[29] The over-compensation for perceived lack of satisfaction of these needs leads to destructive patterns of behaviour. We may tend toward one of these more strongly than another, at times or even permanently. They affect us in very subtle ways: for example, with regard to the spiritual life, we must learn that we cannot grasp hold of or control or manipulate God. Of course we do not think we are trying to control or manipulate God, which is why our attachment to our own emotional programmes for happiness is so subtle. We can cling on to feelings and consolations in prayer because they can give us a sense of getting somewhere in prayer and in our relationship with God. Sometimes God will take these away so that we learn by experience that only God and no gift, no matter how sublime, can satisfy us. So long as these needs are in the dark they will continually influence our lives.

There is nothing at all wrong with liking to be loved and accepted. We would be strange if we did not like that. The same is true of feeling secure and having some control over our lives. These are basic human needs. Unless these needs are met, we shall be out of balance, and our emotional programmes for happiness will seek to compensate. We must recognize this fact, and the very fact of recognition puts balance back in our lives. Our emotional programmes cause a problem only when they secretly and very subtly influence our behaviour to over-compensate for the perceived lack of satisfaction of one of our needs. In that case even people whom we want to help are subtly manipulated by us to feed our needs.

Another aspect of the false self is what has been called cultural conditioning.[30] We are all children of our own culture, and we are heavily influenced by the values of our culture. The term culture in this context can mean one's nation but also any group to which one belongs or has belonged, including school and family. Cultural conditioning begins very early in life as we over-identify with the group that provides us with security, affection, and control. Conformity assures our acceptance in the group, and we can absorb without question the values of the group. We thus acquire preconceived ideas, pre-packaged values, biases, and prejudices.

If I believe that the group to which I belong (family, group of friends, school, university, social class, church, country) is bigger, better, wealthier, or more intelligent than others, I can feel good about myself and secure in the knowledge that I belong. Life naturally brings us into contact with other groups and challenges our preconceived notions, of which we may be unaware. These ideas may be deeply embedded in us and difficult to eradicate, but they affect how we relate to others and our feelings toward the various groups of which we are members. A certain loyalty is natural and good, but when we swallow all the values of our group without examining whether these are actually good in themselves we can tend to be over-loyal and unable to criticize any aspect of the group constructively and so over-react to any perceived criticism.

The emotional programmes are fully in place at an early period in our lives, and so when we reach the age of reason these programmes are not modified by our reason but rather justified, rationalized, and glorified by it. These programmes are infantile in that they are the emotional responses of infants who demand nothing less than instant and constant fulfilment of their needs. They are irrational and obsessive, since we are unaware that they operating within us and so cannot control them. They are addictive, because, whenever the perceived needs are met, needs for bigger and better things arise. They are insatiable, since no symbol can ever fully satisfy our thirst for happiness.

The emotional programming we received in early childhood is unique to each of us. The emotions are the faithful recorders of what is happening inside us. They tell us what our values really are. It has been suggested that we are like computers with vast memories. We store up everything that happens to us from the womb to the present moment. We may not remember the events of early childhood, but the emotions never forget. While the event may be forgotten, the emotional responses are not. They can very easily be retrieved whenever we are in a situation similar to the one that triggered the emotional response in the first place. So when any event that resembles those we once felt to be harmful, dangerous, or rejecting occurs, the same feelings surface, often with a force disproportionate to the situation. Even though we may not have experienced serious traumas, all of us have experienced the emotional fragility of early childhood, and so we bring some deep wounds with us into adulthood as a result. Because of our needs, we tend to seek approval, security, and our sense of well-being from others or from situations, and these can never provide enough of what we want. We are usually not aware that we are doing this, and so it is very difficult to stop.

The most important step of our lives is to recognize that there is something radically wrong. If there is something radically wrong, any superficial change is merely cosmetic. It requires radical surgery. This can be very difficult to accept, especially if we consider ourselves to be rather spiritual people.

St Paul gives a very good description of the profound experience of the religious person who finally accepts that there is something wrong: "I do not understand my own actions. For I do not do what I want, but I do the very thing I hate . . . For I delight in the law of God, in my inmost self, but I see in my members another law at war with the law of my mind, making me captive to the law of sin that dwells in my members. Wretched man that I am! Who will rescue me from this body of death? Thanks be to God through Jesus Christ our Lord!" (Rom. 7:15-24).

When we decide to respond to Christ's call to repentance, to change the direction in which we are seeking happiness, and to take the spiritual journey seriously, we do not start off with a clean slate or clean tape. We have much to do, much reprogramming, which involves first of all finding out what is on the tape by listening to it, then, with the help of God, attempting to clean off those aspects that are obstacles on the spiritual journey. We are dealing with subtle forces that are very powerful. To dismantle the false self system requires more than good resolutions. We need some sort of spiritual discipline such as Centering Prayer, which is designed to help us face the dark side of our personality head-on. As we bring these obstacles gradually into the light, God's love heals and transforms us. This is not just a superficial external change or even only a moral improvement but the beginning of a transformation of our whole personality.

We have a whole set of pre-packaged values and preconceived ideas, which, unless looked at directly and confronted, will be major obstacles to us as we seek to deepen our relationship with God and to live the commandment to love our neighbour as Christ has loved us. Unless we confront these issues we run the risk of being self-righteous and hypocritical—which unfortunately would seem to be an occupational hazard for religious people. Until we face our hidden motivations we cannot act out of the true self but will always filter everything we hear or see through our own needs and wants—the false self.

A discipline such as Centering Prayer slowly softens the blocks of our defence mechanisms, and we begin to see our hidden motives more clearly. It is like turning the light on. The closer we allow God to come to us, the more clearly will we see ourselves. Once we begin to see below the surface, then we can actually start to do something about our false self. This is the road to freedom. St Paul speaks of putting on the armour of God before we engage in the spiritual warfare (see Eph. 6:11-17). The real warfare is against the false self. So the real enemy is not outside of us but within, and this makes the battle much more difficult, because the false self is extremely sneaky. It can dress itself up in any garb; it can appear vulnerable and harmless or whatever—just so that you do not confront it directly.

The false self then is a world of delusion. When we are asked to let go of this self we are being asked to let go of falsity and delusion. Why is it so difficult to let it go? Because it is the only self we know; we believe that if we let go of the false self we will have nothing left. We do not want to admit that we are holding anything back from God, and so the best form of defence is to refuse to accept the idea of the false self or to refuse to see it at work in one's own life. If I do not have a hidden agenda I do not have to do anything about it.

The basic human needs for affection, security, and control have become overwhelming demands that secretly influence even what seem to be our best actions. Our seemingly selfless actions can actually be very selfish. We can attempt to manipulate people and God to fulfil our needs. We are born into a fallen world. We pick up all sorts of values and motives that are not from the gospel but nevertheless shape our behaviour. We are locked into a way of living that does not foster our growth or that of anyone else.

Being a "religious" person—one who goes to church, says prayers, and so on—is no guarantee that the false self system has been put to death. If the false self is evicted from one way of life it simply adapts itself to a new way of life and settles down quite comfortably. The false self is just as much at home in a monastery as in the world of high finance. Remember the monk who fasted all the others under the table! The true self is God-centered and loves others as God loves them; the false self is self-centered and uses the externals of religion not as a means to enter into relationship with God but to bolster itself. The externals of religion can be used as a means of protecting ourselves from God! If we keep on saying our prayers we may not have time to listen to God. If we go to enough religious services we may not feel the need for ongoing conversion. The externals of religion are good in themselves, but they can be adopted by the false self to feed its own desires, so our intention is vital.

It is essential to realize that the false self can operate very subtly. As soon as it thinks it may come under attack, it camouflages itself in order to hide its true nature. There is no better disguise than the religious one. The naked false self is totally self-centered. Fortunately we do not often come across that kind of person. The false self that dresses in religious clothes is much more acceptable but, because of that, much more difficult to spot. Such a person can appear to be very good, observing the externals of religion or being involved in all sorts of Christian service. It is interesting to note that Jesus did not condemn people who committed obvious sins, but he did condemn very religious people whose motives were wrong. Jesus reminded his indignant listeners that prostitutes and tax-collectors would enter the kingdom of heaven before them. What is important is the motive for our religious practices and behaviour. The false self will seek to use even religion to feed its needs for acceptance, security, and power and can do so very subtly.

We must seek to come to grips with our own false self. The first step is to accept the fact that I have a false self and begin to recognize when it is operating. If I do not do that I am wasting my time going on retreat or listening to any sermons and the like, because my false self will act like a tea-strainer, filtering out what it does not want to hear. I will hear what suits me, and if anything seems to be confronting me and asking me to change I will probably become angry. My anger will not seem to be because I have been challenged; I will always find a very good reason for it. I will pick on some trivial point and focus on that or I will hear something that was not said—anything at all will do as long as I do not have to confront myself.

Our greatest friends are our emotions and especially painful ones. What we feel will tell us what our real values are. Do not dismiss your feelings or try to hide them from yourself. It is not a sin to feel; it is human. Admit to yourself what it is you feel: I feel angry; I feel upset; I feel uneasy; I feel happy; I feel very sad. Listen to yourself. Do you ever say, "He has made me angry" or, "she has upset me"? No one has the power to make you feel anything. Something inside you is set off when you feel you are not receiving the esteem you consider your due or the security you need, or when you feel that your control of a particular situation is threatened. There is no commandment that says, "Thou shalt be upset when someone does such and such to you or says something nasty behind your back." Our upset feelings will, however, give us a clue that our motives are not quite as pure as we may have imagined.

When we calm our own inner turmoil, our own emotions, and stop filtering everything through the false self we can begin really to listen to others and to hear what God is saying to us. One of the biggest impediments to spiritual growth is that we are not aware of our motives. The decision to opt for the gospel values does not of itself touch the unconscious motivations that make up the false self. These are firmly in place at a very early age. The influence of the false self extends into every aspect and activity of our lives, including the spiritual, and we are often completely unaware of its effects. We need some sort of spiritual discipline that will actually help us to face our shadow side and become aware of these hidden motives that are directing our lives.

However, a major problem is recognizing when the false self is operating, especially when we are leading a "spiritual life." The false self is so subtle that it will adapt itself quite happily to the spiritual life so long as it is not disturbed. It will still seek happiness through the emotional programmes of esteem, power, and security. I will seek to remain in control of the relationship with God; I will seek esteem in spiritual ways, meaning that I will want people to recognize how spiritual I am; I will get angry when they do not recognize my talents or my towering intellect or my obvious holiness and so on. My Christian service will be about power over people and not about service, and perhaps I will be able to get a glimpse of my true motivation when I examine my reactions to the lack of gratitude or lack of notice for all my work.

The false self is very subtle, and unless we face it head on it will continue to influence our thoughts and actions. Wherever we go, whatever we do, we take our problems with us—the false self shadows us. The gospel asks us to repent—to leave the world of the false self. The gospel challenges us to change the direction in which we are seeking happiness, to look at ourselves and seek to uncover our unconscious motives and bring them into line with the gospel.

Chapter Nine

A DEEPER LOVE

Our deepest desires express a hunger that only God can satisfy.[31] However, in its yearning the human heart gives itself away in slavery to what is not God. In our relationships and through our possessions we seek a fulfillment that is not theirs to give. The heart becomes free only by slowly accepting the invitation of a deeper love. But the danger is that we will use this deeper love in the same way that we have used our other loves—to seek ourselves. God beckons us forward, as it were, but remains always just out of reach. So we let go of other things that may slow us down on our journey. It is this process of letting go that makes us able to receive God. When our hearts are full of many things we have no room for God, but when our hearts are emptied we are ready to be filled with the utter fullness of God.

God must teach us that God is not a thing to be grasped hold of and possessed. And so God hides and we begin to search. In this way God teaches us what love is, and the way we love is transformed. God's love is unconditional and non-grasping. The love of God gives life, and slowly but surely God transforms us if we consent.

Centering Prayer teaches us to let go of control in prayer. At first this may not be very pleasant as we like to be in control of what is happening to us, but as we let go we discover that we are in safe hands—the hands of God. We shall have to cope with various temptations, which are also subtle ways of regaining control. When our prayer becomes dry and even boring we may be tempted to turn back to a way of prayer that made us feel good in the past and where we were in control rather than following wherever God led us. Almost an opposite temptation to be careful of is thinking, when we do experience some peace, "Now I have really arrived. This is contemplation. I am really a contemplative!" We need to let go of this idea also. If we follow any thought we shall be drawn away from our centre, which is God.

Continuing on the inner journey will involve us in a long process whereby God reshapes us according to the image of Christ. The breaking-down of the false self is painful, but the birth of the new self makes all the pain worthwhile. If the chrysalis and the egg could feel, no doubt they would not want to be broken, but without this process there would be no butterfly and no bird. Another term for this process is purification. We are purified so that we can receive God. So on the journey there will be ups and downs, light and darkness, times of strength and times of weakness. We need patience and perseverance as God brings the masterpiece to fruition. Many artists do not like to reveal their work until it is finished. In a way, God is like that. We usually cannot see what God is doing in our lives. Centering Prayer teaches us to let God get on with the work, trusting that God will bring good out of everything.

As we become more conscious of God's presence and work within us as the source of all our happiness we become more ready to dismantle the false motivations we now perceive to be a burden. We have placed our hope for happiness in the false self and now there slowly develops within us a progressive self-forgetfulness and self-abandonment, confident in the power of God to lead us to our full human maturity. We begin to follow God's will not just at the time of prayer but also in daily life.

Sometimes the world seems to mock us in our attempt to seek more than it can give. Even our friends may advise us not to go too far. The search for God and the consequent change that takes place in us has been called "the road less travelled." Searching for the face of the Living God can be a rather lonely business, and it can seem that no one understands us. It is even difficult to understand ourselves: Why are we doing this? Why can we not just settle down and be like everyone else? But there is something deep within us that will not allow us to settle for less than we really desire.

When we really take God seriously, God touches our heart and it is no longer ours. We realize that we cannot find total satisfaction in anything else, but yet God does not immediately respond to our desires. The reason for this is God's desire to transform us. This is where we see the limitation of the human model of friendship for our relationship with God. God indeed desires to have an intimate relationship of friendship with each one of us, but there is more to this relationship. God also acts as healer and consistently works on us to bring about inner healing. Indeed it could be said that God pursues us, seeking in every way to bring us to the fullness of life. Sometimes this healing process can feel like a disintegration, but in faith we are asked to accept that this is indeed part of a process that will lead to the transformation of our humanity.[32] God will not accomplish this work by magic but desires our co-operation. We have to learn a new way of looking at things, a new way of being in the world, and above all a new way of loving. This learning process takes a long time, and it can seem that God has enticed us out into the desert just to leave us there. In fact God has indeed enticed us out into the desert in order to speak to our hearts. The trouble is that when we embark on our journey into the desert to meet God we take with us so many things that slow us down. What slows us down most of all is the false self with all its demands and expectations. Gradually we must let go so that we can continue on our journey unimpeded.

God will call to us in various ways to start out on the journey, and once we have begun God will not give up on us. However, we cannot always understand what God is doing, and at times it can seem that God is completely inactive. We need not be afraid of complaining about this treatment of us, but we also need to trust and believe that God is in fact at work in us and is in the process of creating a masterpiece. For an artist, it does not take long to make a quick sketch, but to make a masterpiece can be a lengthy business.

We have been created with a capacity for God; nothing less than God can ever fully and finally satisfy us, and yet we are forever seeking substitutes for the real thing. We seek the substitutes because we intuitively perceive that the cost of receiving God is not less than everything. Without thinking it through we try to get God on the cheap.

It is one thing to say that we abandon ourselves to God and quite another to live this abandonment out in practice. We have so many subtle ways of deceiving ourselves. We can filter everything through the false self, and so we hear only what we want to hear. I may be distracted during a sermon that challenges me to repent; I can search the scriptures like the Pharisees but not be open to the word of God; I can refuse to accept God's word because it does not come to me in the expected package or from an acceptable person. The spiritual journey requires tremendous honesty, but our honesty produces a reward beyond anything that we could imagine.

Remember the famous example of St John of the Cross: it matters little whether a bird is tied down by a stout cord or a slender thread.[33] It depends on what the bird wants to do. If all it desires is to scrabble about in the dirt around it then being tied does not matter. However, if it wants to fly the cord or thread must be cut. I am attached to my understanding of what is right, to my memory of how God has acted in my life, and to my desire to encounter God. These things can seem to be wonderful and at a certain stage of our journey are indeed wonderful, but there comes a time when they can block further growth. The problem is that the word "my" qualifies them. There is still a very subtle struggle for control. Who will lead the dance and who will follow?

So, who is going to lead the dance? If I have always led and am used to leading, it will be difficult to change my ways. However, if I do change, God will teach me to dance to new music—the silent music of love. At first the music will seem extremely strange and I will stumble and not be at all my usual confident self, but as I gradually learn the steps and become more confident in following my partner a whole new world will open to me. Do I want to explore the strange islands? Do I want to hear the silent music? Or do I want to remain safe? The choice is mine.

Why does God not transform us immediately when we ask for this grace? Remember the story in the Gospel when the two apostles asked Jesus to grant them the favour of placing them at his right and left hand in his kingdom (Matt. 20:21-3). Jesus responded to their request by saying that they did not know what they were asking for. Could they drink the cup that he would drink? They of course responded "yes," but as soon as they had the opportunity to do just that they ran away. It was a long time afterwards, after they had been through the dark night of the passion and the joy of the resurrection, that they were able to drink the cup Jesus offered them.

We understand perfectly that some pain is essential in normal life. People go jogging to maintain their health, despite the fact that it cannot be very pleasant to go out on a cold and wet morning. They go to the dentist and undergo some pain in order to have healthy teeth. They accept injections because they want to go somewhere exotic for their holidays. This sort of pain is so normal that we forget about it because of the purpose we have in view. However, when it comes to the relationship with God, our minds seem to get clouded over. As Job said: "Shall we receive the good at the hand of God and not receive the bad?" (Job 2:10). We seem to expect peace and joy all the time, but that is never-never land. What relationship is always on an emotional high? In the relationship with God we have to grow up, and this is always painful.

Our transformation is the work of God, not our work. All we can do is co-operate with God. According to St John of the Cross, if we wish to be transformed in God we must pass through what he calls "the dark night." The way God destroys the false self and heals the emotional wounds of a lifetime is through the dark night. The dark night is where we walk by faith and the love of God and not by the natural light of human reason. In fact we close our eyes, as it were, to the normal ways of knowing and understanding. This at first makes everything very dark, because our eyes are not yet adjusted to the new way of seeing things, to the way of faith.

The first part of the night is what we can do to co-operate with God. When I take up the spiritual life with great gusto for the first time, and when God really does become very important to me, I can secretly think that I have finally made it. So this is what sanctity is all about! Prayer really flows, and I could spend all day with God, thinking and reading about spiritual things and praying. However, this is only the honeymoon phase of the relationship, and we all know that this stage of human relationships never lasts.

At the beginning of his book on the dark night John details the imperfections of what he calls "beginners."[34] Beginners are those who have made a very good start in their relationship with God. They are very good Christians, but John paints a devastating picture of them, pointing out all their faults. It seems almost cruel. These are good people, but the good is the enemy of the best. What God desires for us is beyond our powers of imagination. To settle for anything less is to settle for second best, for mediocrity. It might not appear to others to be mediocrity; in fact such a person may very well be a pillar of the church, but he or she has accepted far less than God is offering.

Some people think John of the Cross is too hard, too demanding. The reason why he may appear such is that he has experienced God, and this experience is so ravishing, so powerful, that settling for less seems to him utter madness. He would certainly understand the sentiments of St Paul, who said: "I consider that the sufferings of this present time are not worth comparing with the glory about to be revealed to us" (Rom. 8:18). So all the sufferings of the dark night are like labour pains—painful, without a doubt, but for a purpose. If we can understand the purpose, we will endure the pain.

So John points out the imperfections of beginners in order to convince them that although they have undoubtedly made a very good start, it is only a start. They still have a long way to travel, and the sooner they get on the road the quicker they will arrive. The fundamental orientation of beginners is toward themselves. They would of course deny this and indeed be quite upset to think that they might be selfish. But their motive for prayer is the consolation and satisfaction they experience. They in fact measure God by themselves and not themselves by God. The way to know what we are really seeking in prayer is to watch ourselves, how we feel, what we do when prayer becomes an unpleasant duty.

The second part of the night begins when God gradually draws people out of this beginners' state so that they can experience God in the darkness of contemplation. When God sees that someone is responding to grace and becoming detached from sin, God will lead that person further. John says that it is through the delight and satisfaction beginners experience in prayer that they have detached themselves somewhat from worldly things and have gained some spiritual strength. It is at the time when they are going about their spiritual exercises with delight and satisfaction that God suddenly closes the door and stops up the spring of sweet spiritual water they were tasting as often as they desired. God now leaves them in such darkness that they do not know which way to turn. They can no longer use their imagination in meditation. God leaves them in such dryness that they not only fail to receive satisfaction and pleasure from their spiritual exercises and pious works as they used to but also begin to find these things distasteful and bitter.

Everyone experiences periods of dryness from time to time, but these usually do not last long. However, if you are about to enter this phase of the night the dryness just goes on and on and on. Going back to devotions that used to move you will have no effect on the desert of your heart. God, Our Lady, the saints will seem very far from you and to have nothing to do with your life. Reading spiritual books or the Bible will seem like reading the telephone directory. This drying-up of consolation and satisfaction spills over into daily life. You get on with life, but it is as if a dull grey cloud is hanging over everything. In this night we catch glimpses of our real motives, which have usually been hidden from us. The general dryness spills over into daily life, and we may find that we are not as patient, kind, and gentle as we thought.

When I begin to see myself as I really am, it can be a terrible shock. It can seem that I am going backward, that I am getting worse. Many people seem unable to cope with this revelation of self and back off. I can retreat from the personal encounter with God in prayer because it is too demanding. I may very well continue to pray, but my prayer will remain on an external level, and I will not allow God to probe the secret depths of my heart. However, if I go on through this difficult time trusting in God I will gradually become more settled and secure in this darkness. The dark night of St John of the Cross is not always bleak. The night too can be a beautiful time. When our eyes become accustomed to the darkness we can begin to appreciate the beauty. It is only at night that we can see the moon and the stars.

There are some dangers that accompany this phase. Because of this experience, I could give up the spiritual life, give up the search for God as not my cup of tea. It is just too hard. Remember the gospel story about the seed being sown (Matt. 13: 3-8). The seed can actually be wasted; only some of it produces a crop, and the amount of the crop varies. Another danger is that I will seek different ways to divert myself so that I do not have to acknowledge and sit with the pain. The purpose of the night as a whole is to destroy the false self, and the false self will fight back when it is under attack. When satisfaction and consolation from all my usual sources dry up I will try all the harder to get some from them or from other sources. There may begin an almost frantic search for satisfaction. I may very well eat too much, drink too much, read too many trashy novels, watch too much TV, and so on— anything to divert my attention from the real problem. At times we have a tendency to compartmentalize our lives. We may not see any connection between what is happening in our daily lives and what is going on in our prayer. Of course they are intimately connected.

When consolation and satisfaction dry up we tend to complain, but if it is a sign of the onset of this part of the night of sense it is in fact a cause to rejoice. We will not feel like rejoicing, but God is beginning to treat us as grown-ups. A little child hates to be called a baby, so God will not treat us as babies when we are perfectly able to walk. The parents rejoice over the first word or first steps of their child and so God rejoices over us. There would be great concern over a child who refused to walk. God is very much with us at this time, caring for us, watching over our every step. It just seems that God is not there. It feels as if God has gone off somewhere and forgotten to tell us where.

St John of the Cross gives three signs for the authenticity of the onset of the night and the call to contemplative prayer. The first sign that we are being drawn by God from the state of beginners through this night of sense so that we can begin to experience God in the darkness of contemplation is this pervasive dryness and lack of consolation. The second sign, which must go with it, is that we still care deeply for God and begin to think we are not being faithful to God, while all the time we are trying to be. We begin to see ourselves as we really are and see all the little sins and falsities in our lives. We realize the amazing grace that has been poured out on us; we know the immense love that God has for us—and this is how we respond! Of course the just one falls seven times a day, but the person who is being drawn by God is trying very hard to be faithful, while feeling very bad at his or her failures. It is important to try to maintain a sense of proportion and, if possible, a sense of humour in this situation. The third sign is the powerlessness to meditate—the impossibility of using one's imagination and thinking powers to pray. At the same time there is a deep desire simply to be with the Lord without thinking, just being lovingly aware that God is present though not felt. We may perhaps have received a lot from our meditations in the past, from books or our own thoughts about God, but now, despite our best efforts, we cannot complete a meditation. God is feeding such people in a new way, and their palates are not yet accustomed to the new kind of food. Our imagination has done all it can and has sucked everything possible from books and even the Bible at this stage. God's ways are not our ways, and God's thoughts are not our thoughts. Our thoughts cannot confine God, and very soon our imagination can go no further. This can seem to be a disaster because we used to get so much out of thinking about God and from holy meditations.

At such a time I may feel that I cannot pray, since I have no desire to think about anything to do with God and yet have the desire to be with God. Prayer will seem to be a complete waste of time as I feel I am getting nothing out of it, but, strangely, there is the feeling of rightness and peace at a deep level. From time to time this peace will be covered in confusion and anger and all sorts of other feelings, but it will always re-emerge. This peace will give a vague sense that, despite all appearances to the contrary, everything is all right and God is somehow in the midst of this experience.

In the night of sense we begin to perceive that only God can satisfy the desire of the human spirit for unlimited truth, love, and happiness. The dryness and darkness of the night come from our own inner poverty, weakness, and personal sinfulness. We normally feel the absence of God at the time of prayer, and this spreads to other areas of life. There is a tendency to look back longingly for the joys and satisfactions of an earlier period in our relationship with God, but this initial fervour was immature and under the influence of our immature programmes for happiness. In the night of sense God begins to draw nearer. God comes to us from within and not through the external senses or through memory, imagination, or reflection. We need to accept the invitation to realize, in stillness and silence, that though there is dryness God is beginning to communicate with us at a deeper level. Simply being in God's presence at this time is more important than words or pious thoughts.

The night of sense is a phase of transition from a superficial faith toward pure faith. In this night God begins to heal the wounds of our emotional programmes for happiness, which were based on needs that could not be met. The night is designed to bring about the dismantling of these emotional programmes and the death of the false self. The fruit of this purifying process is the freedom to decide what to do without being pushed around by our emotions and compulsions. However, before this freedom comes to us we must accept our own inner poverty, the dark side of our personality; and the fact that God begins to show us very clearly some aspects of our own dark side is one of the principal fruits of the night of sense, although at the time it seems to be anything but a blessing. As children we absorbed many of the values of our culture and education despite the fact that we might have thought we were rebels! In the night these presuppositions are challenged. The very ground on which we always felt secure begins to shake beneath our feet, and a new way of seeing reality opens up before us.

Despite the fact that we may think of ourselves as spiritually mature, we unconsciously carry with us many distorted views of God that come to us mostly from our childhood experiences. These affect how we relate to God, the world, and other people. The night of sense helps us to face our distorted views of God and to let go of them. One way in which God deals with our distorted and limiting views of the divinity is to reduce all our ideas of God to silence. Sometimes this is felt as a loss of the ability to pray or a loss of God. What is actually happening is that God is communicating with us at a deeper level. With time we begin to learn to rest in this silence of God, and this in turn helps us to let go of our emotional programmes and cultural conditioning.

The great temptation during the night of sense is to give up the spiritual journey. The false self will readily supply many good reasons why we cannot go on. If we give up and go away, however, the false self, the cause of most of our problems, goes with us.

God calls to us. If we hear this voice and respond, God will come to us. God begins to change our motivation, and this causes pain. It is a dark night. Through the various phases of the night God secretly teaches us a new way of living and loving. We are being gradually recreated in God's image and gradually conformed to Christ.

As we learn by experience what the love of God really means, the false self begins to die. When we truly realize what is happening in the darkness, that God is transforming us, we can rejoice. The darkness is no longer awful; it becomes a friend:

> Sweeter that night
> Than morning light,
> For Love did loving meet.
> I knew him well,
> And we could dwell
> In ecstasy complete.[35]

It is not at all important for us to know where we are on the journey. Actually it is impossible to know for sure, and it is a sign of spiritual immaturity to be very concerned about this. The relationship with God is based on faith, and the important thing is not for us to have a lot of knowledge about the spiritual journey but actually to be on it, actually to pray. If we really desire that God possess us completely and transform us this will happen, but it will happen in God's time, not ours. It will happen according to God's logic and not ours. We may be the last to know that it is happening, and we may never know on this side of the grave. What does it matter? The only thing that matters is that God's will be accomplished in and through us. We can only do our best and no more. God does not give us desires that are to remain unfulfilled. For these to be fulfilled, however, we must trust in the God who loves us with an everlasting love.

Appendix One

CONTEMPLATIVE OUTREACH

In his book *Intimacy with God* Thomas Keating tells the story of the founding of Contemplative Outreach in the United States as a response to a need expressed by many people.[36] The teaching of the method of Centering Prayer was often enthusiastically received, but many felt the need for some ongoing support for their faith journey. It is to this need that Contemplative Outreach seeks to respond. It is not so much a movement as a network of faith communities, which has spread to many parts of the world. Centering Prayer is a method of prayer that comes out of the Christian contemplative tradition. This tradition—for all sorts of reasons—was nurtured and grew in a mostly monastic setting over the centuries.

The consecrated life is intended to provide the essential structures within which individuals can grow to maturity in their relationship with God. Whether it succeeds or not is another matter. Some elements that seem to foster a maturing prayer life are regular prayer, formation, and community. Does this mean that only members of religious communities can hope to have an intimate relationship with God? A minimum of experience shows that this is clearly not the case. However, religious communities have been around a long time, and and the fact that they have survived so long means that a certain wisdom can be found in the phenomenon of the consecrated life. In order to become mature followers of Christ we need regular encounters with God, we need spiritual formation and education, and we need the encouragement of like-minded people. We also, of course, need to translate our growing relationship with God into some practical love of neighbour. The parish is supposed to be the place where lay Christians receive their spiritual formation and where they experience Christian community, but, once again, experience teaches that this is not always the case. Therefore many groups, organizations, and movements have sprung up to respond to this need and to the thirst very many people have for greater depth in their faith.

It is a truism to state that all Christians are called to holiness. In our day we are witnessing a tremendous upsurge of interest in prayer, especially among lay people. Many are searching for more than their overworked pastors are capable of giving them. Many are searching for greater depth in their prayer. Some have left the traditional Christian Churches that nurtured them because they can no longer find what they are looking for in them. We have witnessed a great interest in Eastern religions and Eastern forms of meditation in recent times.[37] All the time there has been a profound contemplative tradition within Christianity, of which the majority of Christians seem totally unaware. Some stumbled across the tradition in their search to discover the meaning of their experiences. Others, because of lack of knowledge, were either fobbed off with unhelpful and simplistic piety or even sent to a psychiatrist!

Contemplative Outreach encourages every genuine form of contemplative prayer and every discipline that tends toward contemplation but teaches only Centering Prayer and *lectio divina*. A Contemplative Outreach group is intended to support those who feel called to use the Centering Prayer method and who wish to learn more about the Christian contemplative tradition. Just as there are many religious communities in the Church with their own particular characteristics, so also there are many prayer groups, scripture groups, and support groups. While all religious communities will have many things in common, it is clearly absurd to claim that they are all the same in every detail. Jesuits, Carmelites, Dominicans, Cistercians, and others follow different ways to the same goal. In the same way all the various prayer groups differ one from another. The Contemplative Outreach groups or communities offer a shared experience of Centering Prayer and from time to time also of *lectio divina*, as well as some formation regarding the spiritual journey. The reason for setting up these groups in the first place was precisely to form communities of people who wanted to use Centering Prayer as their method of prayer and therefore to provide a support system for them.

Being with like-minded people can be of enormous help to us, but such people or such groups are not always within easy reach. Many people find themselves alone in their search for a deeper life of prayer. Contemplative Outreach, like some other groups, provides a number of different courses and retreats for those who wish to develop their practice of this prayer. Even meeting like-minded people on a rare occasion such as a workshop can be helpful. Those who wish receive training in leading Centering Prayer support groups and in passing on the method of the prayer.

Appendix Two

ACTIVE PRAYERS

The following list is not intended to be exhaustive but merely suggests a few possibilities.

- God, come to my aid
- O Lord make haste to help me
- My God and my All
- Jesus mercy
- My Lord and my God
- Your will be done
- Take Lord and receive
- Bless the Lord my soul
- Lord help my unbelief
- Your will be done
- Your kingdom come

Notes

1. There are many books on the topic of *lectio divina*, but for an excellent and simple introduction, see Thelma Hall, *Too Deep for Words* (New York, Paulist Press, 1988).
2. Guigo II, *The Ladder of Monks and Twelve Meditations*, trans. Edmund Colledge and James Walsh (London, Mowbray, 1978; reprint Cistercian Publications, 1981).
3. *Ibid.*, p. 82
4. See Bernard McGinn, *The Growth of Mysticism*, Vol. II in the series The Presence of God. A History of Western Christian Mysticism (London, SCM Press, 1995), p. 135
5. *Ibid.*, p. 138.
6. St John of the Cross, *The Dark Night*, Bk. I, 10, 6. There are two important translations of the writings of St John of the Cross in English: E. Allison Peers, *The Complete Works of St John of the Cross*, three vols. in one (London, Burns & Oates, 1954; reprint Wheatampstead, Anthony Clarke, 1974); Kieran Kavanaugh and Otilio Rodriguez, O.C.D., *The Collected Works of St John of the Cross*, (Washington, D.C., I.C.S. Publications, 1979).
7. St John of the Cross, *Maxims and Counsels*, 79. St John probably took this saying from Guigo II, *Ladder of Perfection*, chapter 2
8. *Ibid.*, 53
9. See Thomas Keating, *Open Mind, Open Heart* (Shaftesbury, Element Books, 1991), pp. 19-20.
10. St John of the Cross, *Maxims*, 21
11. *Cloud of Unknowing and Other Works*, trans. Clifton Wolters (London, Penguin Books, 1961).
12. Thomas Merton, *Contemplative Prayer* (New York, Image Books, 1990), p.94.
13. For a full history of how the method of Centering Prayer was worked out see Thomas Keating, *Intimacy with God* (New York, Crossroad, 1994), ch. 1.
14. For a discussion of Pope Gregory the Great's teaching on contemplation see Jean Leclercq, François Vandenbroucke, Louis Bouyer, A History of Christian Spirituality, Vol. II, *The Spirituality of the Middle Ages* (London, Burns & Oates, 1968), pp. 3-30; McGinn, *Growth of Mysticism* (n. 4, above), pp. 55-79.
15. *Cloud of Unknowing and Other Works* (n. 11, above), ch. 7, p. 69.
16. See Thomas Keating, *Invitation to Love* (Shaftesbury, Element Books, 1992), for a good explanation of the action of God.

17. St Teresa of Jesus, *Life*, ch. 22, 11, and *Interior Castle*, 7, 4, 8. There are two important translations of St Teresa's writings into English: E. Allison Peers, *Complete Works of St Teresa* (London, Sheed & Ward, 1957) and Kieran Kavanaugh & Otilio Rodriguez O.C.D., *The Collected Works of St Teresa of Avila* (Washington, D.C., I.C.S. Publications, 1976).

18. St Teresa, *Interior Castle*, 6, 10, 7.

19. St John of the Cross, *The Ascent of Mount Carmel*, bk. I, 11, 4.

20. Kahlil Gibran, *The Prophet* (London, Pan Books, 1964), pp. 10-11.

21. I Kings 19:1-18.

22. St John of the Cross, *The Dark Night*, bk. I, 9, 6.

23. John Cassian, *Conferences*, Classics of Western Spirituality, (New York, Paulist Press, 1983), p.132.

24. See Preface of Martyrs I, in the Roman Missal.

25. St Teresa, *Interior Castle*, 7, 4, 15.

26. Matt. 16:24-5. See also Mark 8:34-5 , Luke 9:23-4 and Matt. 10:37-9; Luke 14:26-7

27. Mark 12:28; Matt. 22:38; Luke 10:25-8.

28. For a fuller explanation of these instinctual needs see Keating, *Invitation to Love*.

29. *Invitation to Love*, ch.1.

30. For a fuller treatment of this idea see *Invitation to Love*, ch. 5, "Mythic Membership Consciousness."

31. For an excellent description of this process see John Welch, O.Carm., *When Gods Die* (New York, Paulist Press, 1990).

32. The Christian tradition has often referred to Christ as the Divine Physician. Thomas Keating modernizes this insight and refers to the work of Christ as being like that of an expert psychotherapist and the work of God in us as "The Divine Therapy": see *Intimacy with God*, ch. 8, "The Psychology of Centering Prayer."

33. *The Ascent of Mount Carmel*, bk. 1, 11, 4.

34. *Dark Night of the Soul*, bk.1, chs. 2-7.

35. This translation is by Kathleen Jones, from *Poems of St John of the Cross* (Tunbridge Wells, Burns & Oates, 1993), p. 21.

36. *Intimacy with God*, ch. 1.

37. For a response from the Roman Catholic Church to the use of such forms see *Some Aspects of Christian Meditation*, Letter from the Congregation for the Doctrine of the Faith, 15 Oct. 1989.

Contemplative Outreach U.K.

Provides:
- Networking;
- Assistance and support in establishing local Centering Prayer Programmes;
- On-going Centering Prayer Support Groups;
- Books, Audio and Video Tapes;
- Newsletter;
- Centering Prayer Retreat Director.

If you would like further information on
Centering Prayer and retreats/workshops
or wish to host an Introductory Day, contact:

**The Director
Contemplative Outreach U.K.**

**Tree Tops,
Hoghton Lane,
Nr. Preston,
Lancashire PR5 4ED**

Contemplative Outreach U.K.
1998
Registered Charity No. 1058048

Patrons
Most Rev. Joseph Chalmers, O.Carm.,
Prior General of the Order of Carmelites.

Rt. Rev. Ambrose Griffiths, O.S.B.,
Bishop of Hexham and Newcastle (England)

Centering Prayer Programmes

Introduction to Centering Prayer
- Introductory Workshop teaching the method of Centering Prayer.
- A six-week follow-up programme to help establish a regular practice of Centering Prayer.

Lectio Divina and its movement into Contemplative Prayer
- A workshop emphasizing the Contemplative dimension of scripture.

Centering Prayer Weekend Retreats
- Residential retreats with increased periods of Centering Prayer and continuing education in its conceptual background.

Intensive Retreats
Intended for those with an established practice of Centering Prayer of at least six months to a year.
- Five- or ten-day Silent Residential retreats with increased periods of Centering Prayer and continuing the education in its conceptual background through "The Spiritual Journey" video tape series by Thomas Keating.

Post-Intensive Retreats
- Intended for those who have completed a ten-day Intensive Retreat and wish to further develop their practice of Centering Prayer in a deeper silence.

Facilitator Training and Formation
- Weekend Workshops for those who wish to lead a Centering Prayer Support Group and the first stage for those who are thinking of training as presenters of Introductory Days.

Formation of Contemplative Outreach Service
- A Training Course for Presenters of Introductory Days and anyone else who wishes to deepen their understanding and be of service to Contemplative Outreach, other than as a presenter.